Framing the Media

'Of all human capabilities, it is the capability of expression and communication that is fundamental to our being in a just society. Pamela Philipose in this book takes us through policy and law enacted in the last 75 years of Independence, to help us understand governmental regulation of freedom of speech. From the control of newsprint to the control of digital media, she documents authoritarian tendencies resulting in censorship of free speech. Her contribution will help us shape a better future for the rule of law which cannot exist without free speech.'

Indira Jaising, eminent jurist and
former Additional Solicitor General of India

Policy Studies Series

The Orient BlackSwan 'Policy Studies Series' is designed to fill a visible gap in existing Social Sciences literature: the need to address, empirically investigate and rigorously analyse public policy in the field of governance.

It is important to study the policy world in its entirety because:

- Policies establish the context within which we live out our individual and collective lives and deeply impact the way we and future generations will live and work.
- Policy-making and implementation is a process that is deeply embedded in politics, and serves as an entry point into the politics of a country.
- Public administrators, scholars, journalists, and specialists need to understand the relationship between knowledge systems, technology and the making of policy, the nature of public participation and responses, and how politicians seek to forge networks to ensure that policy is transformed into law.
- Policy-making highlights the linkages between domestic and global contexts. Ideas disseminated through global institutions and civil society networks impact policy-making insofar as they influence identification of problems and propose resolutions.

The literature generated through the Series, we hope, will serve to identify the strength and lacunae of the making of policy and its implementation in India.

The Series Editors

- **Neera Chandhoke** is former Professor of Political Science, University of Delhi.
- **Praveen Jha** is Professor at the Centre for Economic Studies and Planning and Adjunct Professor at the Centre for Informal Sector and Labour Studies, School of Social Sciences, Jawaharlal Nehru University, New Delhi.
- **C. Rammanohar Reddy** is Editor-in-Chief at *The India Forum*, a digital journal-magazine on contemporary issues.

The Series Advisory Board

- **Akeel Bilgrami** is Sidney Morgenbesser Professor of Philosophy, and Professor, Committee on Global Thought, Columbia University, New York.
- **Niraja Gopal Jayal** is Avantha Chair and Professor of Politics at King's College London. She was formerly Professor at the Centre for the Study of Law and Governance, Jawaharlal Nehru University, New Delhi.
- **Prabhat Patnaik** is Editor, *Social Scientist*, and Professor Emeritus, Centre for Economic Studies and Planning, School of Social Sciences, Jawaharlal Nehru University, New Delhi.

Framing the Media

Government Policies, Laws and
Freedom of the Press in India

Pamela Philipose

Orient BlackSwan

All rights reserved. No part of this book may be (i) modified, reproduced or utilised in any form, or by any means, electronic or mechanical, including photocopying, recording or by any information storage and retrieval system, in any form of binding or cover other than in which it is published, without permission in writing from the publisher; or (ii) used or reproduced in any manner for the purpose of training, development or operation of artificial intelligence (AI) technologies and systems, including generative AI technologies, without permission in writing from the copyright holder.

FRAMING THE MEDIA: GOVERNMENT POLICIES, LAWS AND FREEDOM OF THE PRESS IN INDIA

ORIENT BLACKSWAN PRIVATE LIMITED

Registered Office
3-6-752 Himayatnagar, Hyderabad 500 029, Telangana, India
e-mail: centraloffice@orientblackswan.com

Other Offices
Bengaluru, Chennai, Guwahati, Hyderabad, Kolkata,
Mumbai, New Delhi, Noida, Patna

© Orient Blackswan Private Limited 2025
First published 2025
ISBN 978-93-5442-789-3

042301

Typeset in
ITC Berkeley Oldstyle Std 10.5/14
by Le Studio Graphique, Gurgaon 122 001

Printed in India at
Kensington Printing & Packaging, Noida 201 301

Published by
Orient BlackSwan Private Limited
3-6-752 Himayatnagar, Hyderabad 500 029, Telangana, India
e-mail: info@orientblackswan.com

This book is dedicated to all those who have worked and are working to defend, preserve and strengthen freedom of speech in India

Contents

Preface ix
List of Abbreviations xi

Introduction: Media Policy-Making in Independent India   1

1. First Movers on Freedom of Speech and Expression   8
2. A Struggle without End for a Free Press   38
3. Radio, Television and Channelling Changing Ideas   73
4. Freedom of Speech and Expression in the Digital Age   107

Afterword   148

References   150

Preface

Let me start with a bit of personal history. A few months after joining *The Times of India*, Bombay, as a trainee, something weird was unravelling about which I did not have the slightest clue. The newspaper is housed in the distinctive building that earned it the sobriquet of 'Old Lady of Boribunder', and as I walked into the main hall that accommodated its editorial operations, there was an unusual, even uneasy, silence in the air as people went about their tasks with eyes cast down. The hustle and bustle that I had come to associate with that cavernous newsroom was for some reason missing. I asked a colleague what was happening. She replied in hushed tones, 'Emergency has been declared.' Emergency, what's that? Nothing I had learnt in journalism school had prepared me for it. It was the morning of 26 June 1975.

Did the 21 months of the Emergency impart in newspaper editors and workers of the country an understanding of the sometimes-abstruse-sometimes-concrete value of freedom of speech inherent in the constitutional guarantee of Article 19(1)(a)? Did they come to realise how easily, like some inestimably priceless perfume, its essence can evaporate should its container get smashed under the weight of an authoritarian State? It seemed like that was the case: a roaring sea of people emerged on the streets as the results of the 1977 general election were put out on display boards that came up outside newspaper offices. As noted journalist B. G. Verghese, speaking for all the journalists in the country, put it: 'If India won Independence in 1947, it won freedom in 1977.'

The expectation was that Indian journalists, having experienced the Emergency, would never forget what it meant to be unfree. Looking back on that moment of hope in the year 2025, it would appear almost delusional. Not only was the constitutional guarantee of free speech trampled upon, time and again, in the years that followed, a large proportion of the journalistic community allowed itself to betray the basic principles of their profession.

This was one of the reasons why, when Rammanohar Reddy, senior journalist and an editor of the Orient BlackSwan Policy Studies series, invited me to work on a monograph that would view media policies in India through the prism of Article 19(1)(a), I was more than happy to agree.

In the two years that followed, as blank pages filled up, the central theme only seemed to gain in relevance. Over this period a range of individuals, from free speech advocates and human rights lawyers to academics and right to information activists, too numerous to list here, helped immensely to unpack the many dimensions of this subject. My immense gratitude to them, and to my lively family that is never short of opinions—or words!

New Delhi
March 2025

Abbreviations

ABC	Audit Bureau of Circulation
AI	artificial intelligence
AINEC	All India Newspaper Editors Conference
AIR	All India Radio
BARC	Broadcast Audience Research Council
BEA	Broadcast Editors' Association
BJP	Bharatiya Janata Party
BNS	Bharatiya Nyaya Sanhita
CA	Constituent Assembly
ECIL	Electronics Corporation of India Limited
GOI	Government of India
I&B	Union Information and Broadcasting Ministry
IMF	International Monetary Fund
IPC	Indian Penal Code
ISRO	Indian Space Research Organisation
IT	information technology
MIB	Ministry of Information and Broadcasting
MISA	Maintenance of Internal Security Act
NBDA	News Broadcasters & Digital Association
NDA	National Democratic Alliance
NDTV	New Delhi Television Ltd
PMJDY	Pradhan Mantri Jan Dhan Yojana

POTA	Prevention of Terrorism Act
PUCL	People's Union for Civil Liberties
RNI	Registrar of Newspapers for India
RTLM	Radio Télévision des Milles Collines
TADA	Terrorist and Disruptive Activities (Prevention) Act
TRAI	Telecom Regulatory Authority of India
UAPA	Unlawful Activities (Prevention) Act
UNDP	United Nations Development Programme
UNESCO	United Nations Educational, Scientific and Cultural Organization
UPA	United Progressive Alliance
WJA	Working Journalists' Act

Introduction

Media Policy-Making in Independent India

What do we understand by a media and communication policy? The United Nations Educational, Scientific and Cultural Organization (UNESCO) has loosely defined media policy as a set of prescriptions and norms that are meant to guide the actions of communication institutions in a country. The importance of these sets of prescriptions should not, of course, be underestimated because on them are premised the agency and ability of citizens to make democratic choices. But a closer reading of the UNESCO definition would reveal its inadequacies given that not only are media and communication technologies constantly evolving, the contexts and circumstances in which they operate are themselves impermanent. This is why policy-makers have to routinely play catch up or exercise blanket control in anticipation of developments that they read as adverse. It could also explain why, despite a raft of media commissions being set up by the Government of India over the years headed by luminaries like G. S. Rajadhyaksha, P. C. Joshi, Justice P. K. Goswami, or B. G. Verghese, India has not been able to give itself a cogent media policy template. What the country does have is a jigsaw puzzle of policies, rules, regulations, orders and laws related to media and communication technologies. These have been determined by the government's exigencies and intentions which, if challenged, have then been interpreted by the courts.

Here we seek to understand the forces that have driven these interventions in post-independence India, and the interests that have undergirded them, focusing on the policy-making of the central government, rather than those generated at the level of states. Although the Union government purports to speak and act for the people of the country, we know it is never neutral. Abigail Levin, a professor of philosophy, has argued that the State's enactment of the law is 'always a felicitous illocutionary speech act, which carries an in-built claim to the truth as it produces self-validating rules that have instantaneous binding effects upon an individual's behaviour ... it sets the rules for all further discourses within the society' (cited in Gaur 2023).

A benign interpretation of these rules and laws on speech and expression would maintain that they were steered by the central government's desire to ensure universal access to the benefits of media and communication resources for all its citizens, based on the presumption that the country's mass media helps to instil the idea of Indian nationhood in the minds of its citizens.

Periodic averments from the Union Ministry of Information and Broadcasting (I&B) have only emphasised this. When the Prasar Bharati Act of 1990, for the creation of an autonomous public service broadcaster, came into force in 1997, a document from the I&B Ministry provided a good sampling of such intentions. It promised, among other things, that Prasar Bharati would safeguard citizens' rights to be informed freely and objectively; facilitate a fair and balanced flow of information including divergent views without promoting any ideology; and uphold the unity and integrity of the country and the values enshrined in the Constitution (Prasar Bharati 2020). It is another matter that none of this happened because the autonomy promised for Prasar Bharati never materialised.

A more realistic assessment of media policy-making over the years would therefore necessarily factor in more pragmatic considerations on the part of the State and changes in its ideological stance, since it is well-recognised the world over that media, communication tools and strategies as well as media policies are always inseparable from the State's ideological framework. The history of such policy-making also reveals that despite claims that the laws, rules and regulations drawn up for various media aim to protect 'national interest', they are invariably oriented towards the self-protection and the self-aggrandisement of the governments, political leaders and ruling parties in power at that particular point of time. As one media observer put it, 'Perhaps, the idea of having guidelines, and not a definite policy, was to provide room for manoeuvring and manipulating the media according to the convenience of the powers that be' (Prasad 1996: 47).

Examples abound of such self-serving policy responses, most specifically in times when authoritarian populism rises against a backdrop of citizens asserting their right to free speech. The national emergency declared by Prime Minister Indira Gandhi witnessed a welter of media policies that sought to buttress her broader political agenda of State capture and control. Liberalisation of the economy and globalisation in 1991 caused the final rupture of what came to be known as the Nehruvian consensus that privileged democracy, secularism, welfarism, socialism and non-alignment within a 'framework of rules, institutions and conventions' (Rajni 1961). It was driven by a spate of economic and political developments, including a sharp rise of fuel prices during the first Gulf War (1990–1991), the plummeting of remittances into the country from the Middle East, capital flight and a balance of payments problem, all leading to a bankrupted economy. The impact liberalisation had on the media was stark and immediate and it swept away the earlier notion of journalism as a public service. Today, we have a government under the National Democratic Alliance (NDA) led by PM Narendra Modi, with its ethno-nationalist politics and neoliberal policies, which is paying extraordinary attention to evolving ways to crimp media autonomy.

In the pages that follow, we will be considering all these phases. But what needs to be iterated here is that media policy from the earliest days of the Indian republic has often been an extension of executive fiat.

Here then is the paradox that has always governed such policy-making in India. On the one hand, we have the existence of a 'free and fair' media widely acknowledged as a benchmark of the country's deliberative democracy in the Habermasian sense, where citizens, enabled by the unique power bestowed on them by media and communication technologies, can participate as equals in the public sphere. On the other, we have the State attempting through its policy-making to control media functioning and, by extension, national conversations and the shaping of public opinion.

There is another factor that has to be considered here: the power of the market, which has played a singular role in shaping media policy in this country. Over the years, the government's ideological orientation has determined whether its media policies sought to resist the suzerainty of big capital over the country's media or encourage the conscious embracing of it.

To move from the post-independence phase, when the State embraced a developmental model based on a planned allocation of resources within a mixed economy, to the period of neoliberalism ushered in during the early 1990s, is to visit a completely new landscape. Under the impact of globalisation and deregulation that the New Economic Policy of 1991 enabled, the idea of a Nehruvian consensus premised on secularism, welfarism, socialism and non-alignment within a 'framework of rules, institutions and conventions' (Rajni 1961) finally disintegrated. Given the close interlinkages between economic policy and media policy, it was only inevitable that the economic restructuring that took place following a severe debt crisis would also witness major transformations within the sphere of media and communication.

Nothing reflected this more than the slow attenuation of State-run Doordarshan and the deregulation of the television industry. Despite the State trying hard to incorporate electronic media into its overall 'developmental' vision for the media from the Sixth Five Year Plan to the Eight Five Year Plan—a period stretching from 1980 to 1997—by the late 1990s, the State's Ninth Five Year Plan (1997–2002) formally acknowledged that although Doordarshan had the biggest terrestrial broadcasting network in the emerging electronic media scenario, it was no longer 'the sole provider of TV broadcast service in the country'.[1]

The deregulation of television media was anything but smooth and the ensuing policies did not amount to a new cohesive regulatory order but a 'statist patchwork of overlapping, confusing and contradictory controls that emerged not out of any grand post-reform design, but out of that utterly untranslatable north Indian term word jugaad (meaning to somehow get by and manage)' (Mehta 2015: 104).

Confusion and contradiction continued to mark media policy-making well into the age of the internet. As neoliberal capitalism forged new markets, increased the pace of technological change and ushered in new patterns of media consumption, it profoundly altered the nature of journalism in the country and the manner citizens approached the media. What is striking about the new patterns of media consumption was the way they reinvented—not replaced—old traditions, legacies and shibboleths and made them available to newer audiences. The reimagining of Hinduism as Hindutva in the current era is a case in point.

This monograph will examine some of the important policies regulating the media and media practices in independent India. Chapter 1 looks at the tropes concerning freedom of speech and expression during the Constituent Assembly debates. It dwells on the manner in which the founding fathers and mothers of the republic envisaged media freedoms and the manner in which the newly independent country went about mainstreaming some of the core values and principles that emerged from that process.

This is followed in Chapter 2 with a brief overview of policy-making that has impacted print media, from the later days of Jawaharlal Nehru to those of his daughter, Indira Gandhi. Chapter 3 will examine the period leading up to economic liberalisation and globalisation and their impacts on the media in general and television in particular. The last section, Chapter 4, takes note of the fact that, unlike the case of legacy media like print and television, digital media grew in parallel with the emergence of economic liberalisation and globalisation. While media policies now focused more closely on the internet and digital media, the ambit of State policy-making often extended to all the avatars of the media, in an effort at inter-media agenda setting that was driven by an impulse to control the media in general.

One of the most important constitutional guarantees that this country has, one that was widely discussed during the Constituent Assembly debates, is freedom of speech and expression. Consequently one of the most efficacious touchstones for evaluating a media policy is to pose the question of whether it furthers the democratic exercise of the freedom of speech and expression, or impedes it.

This is a question that will emerge time and again as we consider seven decades of media policy-making in the country.

Note

1. See the 9th Five Year Plan, vol. 2 (1997).

one

First Movers on Freedom of Speech and Expression

British colonialists recognised very early that ruling a country as large and as variegated as India would require control over its public sphere and press. Interestingly, Indian rulers before them had actively discouraged the use of the printing press because it had threatened their authority, and this has been offered by British historian C. A. Bayly as a reason for the 'late start of printing' in India (Bayly 1999: 200). However, Bayly goes on to argue, drawing from Benedict Anderson's thesis about print capitalism, that 'it is difficult to imagine the emergence of mature nationalism without the prior spread of the printing press and the newspaper' in India (ibid.).

By the late eighteenth century, it was increasingly difficult for power-wielders of the Company Raj to ignore the growing tribe of pen pushers. James Hicky, publisher of *Hicky's Bengal Gazette*, India's first English-language newspaper, offered salacious tidbits about those in power and corrupt stalwarts like Governor-General Warren Hastings had much to fear from his poison pen. But it was not until nearly two decades later, in 1799, that the first official law to keep the press in check—Censorship of Press—was passed, ostensibly to fob off the threat of a French invasion.

According to historians, British rulers were in two minds about the press. While they wished to instrumentalise contemporary publications to gain insights into Indian society and find opportunities to promote 'enlightenment values', they were also wary about the consequences of allowing them a free rein. Some governors-general were more liberal than others. While Lord Bentinck (1833–35) wanted to allow the growth of the indigenous press, his successor, the Earl of Auckland (1836–42), was anxious that just about anything, including seditious material, could be pushed into the newsletters that were in circulation. A contemporary newspaper, *Friend of India*, observed that the colonial empire was an empire of opinion, but that opinion could be destabilised at any point.

British Empire as an 'Empire of Opinion'

Two elements went into the British endeavour to build an 'empire of opinion'. *First*, the creation of its own information order. The appointment of an India Office Information Officer in May 1921 (Kaul 2003: 151) would indicate that by the early twentieth century this system was firmly in place. *Second*, the promulgation of a diverse range of laws ranging from Customs Acts (to prevent the transmission of selected published material by post) to the law against sedition.

It is striking that these laws were often an immediate response to perceived resistance from the 'native' population. The Indian press and public opinion sparked incessant worry at the highest levels of the occupying power. In 1823, press regulations made it mandatory for all publications edited by Indians to acquire licences to both publish and to circulate the material they published. Amidst the turmoil of the 1857 uprisings, that law was further amended to empower the government to halt the publication and distribution of any printed matter.

Once India came under the British Crown, this suspicion of local sentiments only deepened: 'Various surveillance and censorship protocols introduced after the convulsions of 1857 were consolidated in 1867 by the Press and Registration of Books Act, which required that three copies of all publications be deposited with local government' (Pinney 2012: 30). Later, as the Second Anglo-Afghan War (1878–80) raged and agricultural riots broke out in the Deccan, all of which were reported in the local press, the British Raj enacted The Vernacular Press Act of 1878 (ibid.). The particularly repressive provisions of this law, which allowed the government to issue search warrants and raid the premises of newspapers without judicial assent, were aimed solely at the newspapers in non-English languages. It is said that resentment against this draconian law provided a fillip to the incipient nationalist sentiments of the late nineteenth century.

To drive every seditious thought from the mind of every Indian was what laws of this kind sought to do. In 1870, sedition was expressly introduced as Section 124 A of the Indian Penal Code (IPC), which had already come into force in 1860. The wording of this new section made it clear that repressing newspapers deemed seditious was one of the prime motivations behind the enactment: 'Whoever, by words, either spoken or written, or by signs, or by visible representation, or otherwise, excites or attempts to excite disaffection towards, the Government….' The immediate reason for such a provision was continuing 'Wahabi' influence on the Indian population. These mass religious preachers who often advocated rebellion were perceived as one of the triggers for the uprising of 1857.

The 'natives', in the eyes of their colonial masters, were framed as an impetuous, unthinking lot, susceptible to rumour-mongering and prone to violent responses. In 1898, the law was made more stringent after Bal Gangadhar Tilak was hauled up in court for publishing detailed reports in his magazine, *Kesari*, of the Shivaji Coronation Festival, where references had been made to 'swarajya' (self rule). The case, *Queen Empress v. Bal Gangadhar Tilak*, 1897, invited national attention. The following year Article 124 A was broadened and made more stringent (Saksena and Srivastava 2014).

If swarajya was anathema to the rulers, so was the Swadeshi Movement that focused on resisting British-made goods. It was against this backdrop that the colonial government passed the Newspaper (Incitement to Offences) Act in 1908, followed by the Indian Press Act of 1910, which introduced a security deposit for establishing a printing press. This amount could be forfeited should the entity fail the test of obedience to the Raj. The Home Member Herbert H. Risley, in a speech made before the law was introduced, made this abundantly clear: 'Everyday the Press proclaims, openly or by suggestion or allusion, that the only cure for the ills of India is independence from foreign rule ...' (Pinney 2012: 31).

As the years passed and as the popular imagination in the country was seized by the idea of 'independence from foreign rule', the need to hold the press in check became even more manifest. The Anarchical and Revolutionary Crimes Act, or the Rowlatt Act, passed in February 1919, virtually meant that wartime legislation—namely the Defence of India Act passed in 1915 in the midst of World War I—was to continue even in peacetime, with all its draconian provisions including censorship of the press and abridgement of people's right to freedom of speech and expression. Outrage against the new law assumed pan-national proportions. A non-violent satyagraha against the law, led by Gandhi, was to be one of the triggers for the unconscionable massacre of unarmed people at Jallianwala Bagh in 1919. The

British Indian Army and General Dyer in particular were seen as responsible for this brutal response.

Reportage on the massacre was strictly censored and it required the courage of journalists like Benjamin Guy Horniman, editor of the *Bombay Chronicle*, to defy official strictures and publish a report in his paper. The wrath of the State soon descended on him. He faced two years of rigorous imprisonment, the suspension of his newspaper and deportation to Britain (Arshi 2019). But Horniman managed to smuggle photographs of the massacre which were then published in a prominent British newspaper, leading to widespread condemnation of the colonial regime back home.

As World War II broke out in 1939, the Defence of India Act and Rules, 1939, made their appearance. A historian, commenting on wartime censorship, argued that it had two pillars:

> The first consisted of provision[s] predating the war (the CrPC, the IPC, the Sea Customs Act, the Press Act of 1931, and so on); the second (the Defence of India Act and Rules) were issued as wartime measures. They had provisions to pre-censor certain articles.... The Official Secrets Act was amended too, and its violation invited the death penalty or transportation for life. (Sethi 2019: 125)

Tryst with Freedom: Was it Really a Dawn?

The Constituent Assembly (CA) proceedings began in December 1946 within the framework envisaged by the Cabinet Mission Plan of the British government. The Muslim League stayed away, which meant that a quarter of the nation at that time remained unrepresented. The Assembly therefore chose to self-define its relevance by arrogating to itself the authority to control its own existence.

Its second and third sessions, held in April and July 1947, took place under the shadow of Partition which saw at least a million perish. Until that point, the CA did not have the sanction of the law. It was only once the Indian Independence Act came into force on 15 August 1947, during the CA's fourth session, that it gained independent legal status. Six other sessions were to be convened thereafter, ending with the 11th session of November 1949, which saw the formal adoption of the constitutional document.

The debates that took place within the CA were like the country imagining its future by talking to itself. It was the members of this august assembly who attempted the first framing of freedom of speech and expression as a valued constitutional right. Granville Austin (1966) describes the backdrop against which these debates were conducted, over the course of 165 days between December 1946 and November 1949. This was a period that saw riots breaking out in the north and east of the country, the arrival of refugees, disasters like the Kanpur floods, and an attack by Pakistan near Poonch (ibid.: 44–45). Not only did Jinnah die during the span of the CA debates, Gandhi was assassinated in January 1948, leading to the trial of Nathuram Godse. The 'very stained light' of Partition, in Faiz Ahmed Faiz's words, cast a dark shadow over the Assembly's discussions. Paul Brass echoed Granville when he observed that India's republican Constitution was born more in fear and trepidation than in hope and inspiration (Brass 2000: 60).

While freedom of speech of all Indians was an article of faith for the national movement and the erstwhile freedom fighters, the onerous task of ruling a country of 340 million weighed heavy on the new leaders. A speech made by Vallabhbhai Patel in the year before independence, when he was the Home Member and the Member for Information and Broadcasting, provides evidence of the change in attitude that came with the switch in responsibility and status. Patel, who was to soon become independent India's first Home Minister and Deputy Prime Minister, was careful with his words in that speech of 14 October 1946: 'The Press must have unfettered freedom in the presentation of news and expression of views, but it also has the obligation to preserve the integrity of the State and support the legitimate activities of a popular Government' (Sethi 2019: 178).

Before coming to how freedom of expression came to be envisaged during the Constituent Assembly debates, there was the more foundational aspect of how freedom itself was to be perceived. That was one of the big questions before the Constituent Assembly. Jawaharlal Nehru moved the resolution that brought the CA into being during its first session, which began in December 1946. The fifth point raised in the resolution recognised, among other things, that there was to be 'freedom of thought, expression, belief, faith, worship, vocation, association and action, subject to law and public morality'.[1]

Very early on, members of the CA also recognised that the freedom of the country depended crucially on the freedom of speech and expression, which in turn depended on other guarantees like freedom of movement in order to be made more viable. The United Nations (UN) charter of human rights, which was ratified on 10 December 1948, was also referenced in the discussion.[2] One member spoke for many in the Assembly on 2 December 1948, while Article 13 was being discussed: 'I regard freedom of speech and expression as the very life of civil liberty, and I regard it as fundamental.' He saw it as a hard-fought-for outcome that the people of India had arrived at after many struggles against the colonial rulers.[3]

The backdrop of communal violence, and Partition in particular, was a constant point of reference, yet some members had the courage to argue against succumbing to the anxieties caused by memories of the blood-letting. One member put it thus: 'These sad memories should be left to the limbo where they deserve to remain. We have no doubt the unfortunate experiences in which individuals moved by whatever sentiments have tried to exert violence and do injury to their fellows which no civilised State can put up with.' Yet, he went on to suggest, the 'Constitution should be framed, not for these abnormal situations, but normal situations and for reasonable people who it must be presumed will be normally law-abiding.'[4]

Ultimately, however, the argument in favour of greater strictures won the day; the idea that idealism had to be tempered by pragmatism triumphed. Lawrence Liang argues that if Article 19(1)(a) can be interpreted as an attempt to create a space of deliberative democracy, albeit a limited one:

> It is at best a partial project where the deliberative nature of the reason underlying it is also accompanied by a sense of a nervous public sphere exemplified in Article 19(2), where the full citizen and the infantilised citizen occupy the same sphere. (Liang 2016: 819)

Wrestling with Sedition

The struggle to preserve the 'spirit of the Constitution' kept raging and one of the interesting battles in the Constituent Assembly was over the law of sedition. The version that came up for discussion on 1 December 1948 made the following exceptions to freedom of speech and expression:

> Nothing in sub-clause (a) of clause (1) of this article shall affect the operation of any existing law, or prevent the State from making any law, relating to libel, slander, defamation, *sedition* or any other matter which offends against the decency or morality or undermines the authority or foundation of the State.

This caused some disquiet, especially over the retention of the law of sedition. One member stood up and stated, 'If full civil liberties subject to Police Powers, are to be allowed to the people of this country, all laws of a repressive character including the Law of Sedition will have either to go or to be altered radically....'[5] What followed was an amendment to remove the word 'sedition'. While moving an amendment along these lines, K. M. Munshi noted that his amendment 'seeks to delete the word sedition and uses a much better phraseology, viz. "which undermines the security of, or tends to overthrow, the State"' (Constituent Assembly Debates 1948a). When the NDA-II government sought to 'de-colonise' the criminal justice system by bringing in the Bharatiya Nyaya Sanhita (BNS) Act in 2023 to replace the Indian Penal Code, it dropped the word 'sedition' but brought in new language—'acts endangering sovereignty unity and integrity of India'—to punish the same crime under Section 150 (BNS).

A cosmetic change it may have been, but nevertheless the decision to drop the term 'sedition' from the draft Constitution was widely applauded. It is another matter that 'sedition' remained in the Indian Penal Code and was declared, 14 years later, to be constitutional by the Supreme Court (*Kedar Nath Singh v. State of Bihar*, 1962). It took another seven decades and more for the apex court to argue, in 2022, that it should be dropped from the statute books altogether. Yet the political executive and police force seem loath to see the end of that law. In 2023, the Law Commission came up with a report recommending retaining the offence and making punishment for it more stringent (Bhatia 2023).

During the CA debates, many expressed trust in the government of the day to take its responsibilities as protector of people's rights seriously. According to one member of the

Constituent Assembly, the government was 'utterly incapable of doing any wrong to the people'.[6]

Citizens of the country today should be grateful to those who resisted going along with this argument blindly. The due diligence paid to each word and phrase was admirable and valuable. A term like 'reasonableness' was brought into the picture in the context of restrictions to the guarantees, and there was debate even on the phrase 'freedom of speech and expression', as the following observation would indicate:

> I do not know what type of freedom of speech the draftsman had in mind when he adds to it the freedom of expression separately. I thought that speech and expression would run more or less parallel together. Perhaps 'expression' may be a wider term, including also expression by pictorial or other similar artistic devices which do not consist merely in words or in speech.[7]

Press Freedom Synonymous with Free Speech?

Particularly important for purposes of this book was the question of whether freedom of the press should be guaranteed as a constitutional right separately or whether it is inherent in the guarantee of freedom of speech and expression. The revolutionary potential of Article 19(1)(a) comes into view when you contrast it with what existed earlier. India, before it became independent, was bereft of any statutory guarantee—forget constitutional guarantee—of the kind envisaged in this article. There were court verdicts like the oft-cited 1914 judgment pronounced by the Privy Council (*Channing Arnold v. King-Emperor*) that saw the freedom of the journalist as coterminous with the freedom of the subject. But case law, while being an important marker of jurisprudence, lacks the iteration of fundamentals that is inherent in constitutional law.

The members of the Constituent Assembly understood well the malefic effects of colonial laws on the right of expression of the press. In fact, among the first review exercises that the newly independent Indian State had undertaken was to set up a committee to thoroughly scrutinise existing press laws, including the Official Secrets Act (1923) and the Indian Press (Emergency Powers) Act (1931). The report of this committee came out in May 1948 even as the Constituent Assembly debates were underway. Initial discussions on Article 13 (which as we saw later became Article 19) sought for it the broadest definition of what constituted freedom of expression. According to one member, Damodar Swarup Seth, it was to include not just freedom of the press as a separate guarantee from 'freedom of speech and expression' but 'secrecy of postal, telegraphic and telephonic communications'. He went on to say,

> I think, Sir, it will be argued that the freedom is implicit in clause (a), that is, in the freedom of speech and expression. But, Sir, I submit that the present is the age of the Press and the Press is getting more and more powerful today. It seems desirable and proper, therefore, that the freedom of the Press should be mentioned separately and explicitly. (Constituent Assembly Debates 1948a)

His colleague K. T. Shah fleshed out the argument further in an amendment to the text presented soon after which included the freedom of the press. Shah observed that the question of freedom of the press has sparked the greatest, most bitter constitutional struggles in every country where a liberal constitution prevails, yet it has come to be enshrined in those constitutions. His amendment stated that 'Subject to the other provisions of this article, all citizens shall have the right—(a) to freedom of speech and expression;

of thought and worship; of press and publication....' Second-guessing the drafters, he agreed that there have been instances where the press has gone beyond its legitimate limits but legal provisions could be introduced to check this. He reiterated that he could not imagine why such experienced draftsmen felt it necessary to leave the freedom of the press to the 'charity of the administrators of the Constitution when occasion arose to include it by convention or implication, and not by express provision'. To omit this provision, he insisted repeatedly, would prove to be a 'great blemish which you may maintain by the force of the majority, but which you will never succeed in telling the world is a progressive liberal constitution, if you insist on my amendment being rejected' (Constituent Assembly Debates 1948a).

It was, as he had feared, rejected, as were other proposed amendments that included the guarantee of freedom of the press. Attempts were made to mount pressure on B. R. Ambedkar, as chair of the Drafting Committee, to bring in an amendment to include freedom of the press as a sub-clause in Article 13. Some pointed out that the exclusion of the media from the section on right to freedom of expression actually marked a reversal of Ambedkar's own position on the issue. A book he had authored in 1945, and submitted to the Constituent Assembly in 1947 on behalf of the All India Scheduled Castes Federation, entitled *States and Minorities: What are Their Rights and How to Secure them in the Constitution of Free India*, had stated explicitly: 'No law shall be made abridging the freedom of the press, of association and of assembly except for consideration of public order and morality.'[8] An Assembly member, while recalling this, remarked that within a year Dr Ambedkar was 'so changed that he now placed so many restrictions in the Article' (Constituent Assembly Debates 1948b).

Ambedkar, however, defended his position against specifically mentioning the media in the Article on freedom of expression, maintaining that it was unnecessary as the press and the individual or citizen were the same. The editor or manager of the press, he argued, is a citizen who can exercise free speech (Kruthika 2020). In the final analysis, to him what mattered was the manner in which the Constitution and its guarantees were safeguarded. In his last address to the Constituent Assembly he expounded on this view:

> … however good a Constitution may be, it is sure to turn out bad because those who are called to work it, happen to be a bad lot. However bad a Constitution may be, it may turn out to be good if those who are called to work it, happen to be a good lot. (Emmanuel 2018)

Many within the Drafting Committee were driven by a profound suspicion of the press of the day. This became clear soon after the Constitution of India, the document that the CA had worked so hard on over the course of three years, became a reality in 1950. The Supreme Court of India, shortly after the new Constitution had come into force, was called upon to pronounce on two notable cases involving publications which happened to espouse politically opposite views, and it went on to forcefully uphold the right of freedom of expression for the press. Romesh Thapar's *Crossroads* with its leftwing orientation had been subjected to a ban; while the rightwing *Organiser*, edited by K. R. Malkani, was asked to submit itself for pre-publication scrutiny to check for partisan journalism.

In two separate judgments, the apex court declared that the public safety acts cited to ban or restrict these publications went against the sanctity of Section 19(1)(a) as well as the Supreme Court's own role as 'the protector and guarantor of fundamental rights'. The ban against *Crossroads*, it pronounced, had contravened Section 19(1)(a) even if the exceptions granted in 19(1)(b) were to be considered; while in the case of *Organiser*, the court ruled that there were no constitutional provisions for pre-censorship. These verdicts turned out to be a template for high courts across India which, following the Supreme Court's arguments, went on to 'strike down a range of other speech-restrictive laws: the Press (Emergency Powers) Act of 1931, as well as the sedition clause of the Indian Penal Code' (Burra 2019).

Simultaneously, the press also turned very critical of the government in its handling of various instances of civil unrest, including the flow of refugees into West Bengal. Any attempt to clamp down on adverse media comment was deemed unconstitutional by the courts. According to historian Tripurdaman Singh, the new Constitution, with its fundamental rights guarantees, created new forms of contestation with the State: 'zamindars, businessmen, editors and concerned individuals had repeatedly taken the central and state governments to court over their attempts to curtail civil liberties, regulate the press, limit upper-caste students in universities and acquire zamindari property'. The courts, he noted, 'struck mighty blows against the government'.[9]

First Amendment of the Constitution

For the rulers, this state of play was clearly unsettling, especially because it jeopardised the social reform agenda envisaged by Nehru and his ministerial colleagues to which the largely conservative press of the day was opposed. Within the span of a few months, the Government of India (GOI), under Nehru, intervened to counter such excessively literal, even liberal, interpretations of the Constitution on part of the judiciary, and discipline the press, among other aims. Three major steps were envisaged to get the press to fall in line: a constitutional amendment later known as the first amendment came into force in 1951; the Press (Objectionable Matter) Act was passed in 1951; and a Press Commission under Justice G. S. Rajadhyakhsa was set up the following year.

The constitutional amendment introduced changes in Article 19(2) and declared that nothing in Article 19(1)(a) was to affect the operation of any law that imposed 'reasonable restrictions' in the interests of preserving 'public order', or preventing 'incitement to an offence', or for the sake of friendly relations with foreign states. In the earlier formulation, the grounds were limited to libel, slander and defamation, contempt of court and anything 'that undermined the security of the state or tended to overthrow it'.

Responding to this move, a group of members from across the political spectrum, including those ideologically aligned with the Hindu right like S. P. Mookerjee of the Hindu Mahasabha, as well as socialists like J. B. Kripalani and Jayaprakash Narayan, put out minutes of dissent. Mookerjee in his minute of dissent argued that the government had not sufficiently established the requirement for such changes and the way it had gone about the amendment amounted to denying the Constitution 'its inherent sanctity and sacredness' (*Hindustan Times* 2022). Three members, K. T. Shah, Sardar Hukam Singh and Naziruddin Ahmad, jointly submitted that an amendment of this kind was premature since the Constitution had only recently come into force, while N. Kunzru in his dissent note pointed out that the government had not established 'any clear and convincing case for the proposed amendments' (ibid.). He too decried the attempt of the government to rush these amendments through when the Constitution had been in force for only 16 months.

Nehru countered this in his address to Parliament on 29 May 1951 by arguing that 'if something is necessary, then it does not matter whether it is 16 months or 16 weeks'.[10] Nehru had always seen himself as committed to a free press. Just six months earlier, in an address to the All India Newspaper Editors' Conference, he had stated forcefully,

> To my mind, the freedom of the Press is not just a slogan from the larger point of view but it is an essential attribute of the democratic process. I have no doubt that even if the government dislikes the liberties taken by the press and considers them dangerous, it is wrong to interfere with the freedom of the Press.... I would rather have a completely free Press with all the dangers involved in the wrong use of that freedom than a suppressed or regulated Press. (SARJAC n.d.)

This espousal was to be in sharp contrast to his response to the minutes of dissent, in which he critiqued the functioning of the press even as he was at pains to clarify that the intention behind the amendment was not to suppress the press: 'When we brought forward these amendments, any desire to curb or restrain the press, generally speaking, was exceedingly far from our minds.... We are dealing with a particular situation ... a situation that grows more difficult for a variety of reasons, national and international'. The threat to freedom of expression could also come from interests which sought to control the press, he argued.

On each of the newly introduced restrictions he had something to say. On the insertion of 'public order' to restrict freedom of speech, he stated,

> We talk of the freedom of the Press. What exactly does it mean, I ask. So much freedom of the Press we have got today. But the freedom only means suppression or lack of suppression by Government authority. When huge Press chains spring up preventing the individual freedom of the Press, when practically the Press in India is controlled by three or four groups of individuals, what is that Press?[11]

Arguing that reasonable restrictions were valid when it came to friendly relations with foreign governments, he asked, 'Suppose you do something which seems to us to incite to war, do you think we ought to remain quiet and await the war to come?' In other words, he said, if the press wanted freedom of expression, it needed to exhibit 'some balance of mind which it seldom possesses.... They cannot have it both ways—no balance and freedom'.[12]

Twelve years later Article 19(2) was amended for the second time, with one more restrictive clause added: 'sovereignty and integrity of India'. It now reads: '(2) Nothing in sub clause (a) of clause (1) shall affect the operation of any existing law, or prevent the State from making any law, in so far as such law imposes reasonable restrictions on the exercise of the right conferred by the said sub clause in the interests of the sovereignty and integrity of India, the security of the State, friendly relations with foreign States, public order, decency or morality or in relation to contempt of court, defamation or incitement to an offence.'

To be noted here is the fact often pointed out by defenders of free speech—that the phrase 'reasonable restrictions' in this Article has not received the attention that it warrants.

As Gautam Bhatia, a theorist of constitutional freedoms, observed, while Article 19(2) contains an eclectic mix of content-neutral and content-based restrictions, the precise nature of which depends heavily upon judicial interpretation, the question remains: 'what principles determine the content—or communicative messages—that may be legitimately regulated by the government? Is some speech more valuable than other speech? Should certain kinds of speech be given greater protection than other kinds?' (Bhatia 2016: 38). The answer, he went on to say, depends on what society considers to be free speech, which leads to another question: 'Is there a central purpose to free speech, so that speech fulfilling this purpose is entitled to maximum protection, while other kinds of speech are relegated to the background?' (ibid.). That question has largely remained unanswered in contemporary India.

The Constitution (First Amendment) Act brought about a raft of changes including validating laws that abolished zamindari, but arguably its most important aspect was with regard to qualifying freedom of speech guarantees. According to its Statement of Objects and Reasons, 'The citizen's right to freedom of speech and expression guaranteed by Article 19(1)(a) has been held by some courts to be so comprehensive as not to render a person culpable even if he advocates murder and other crimes of violence. In other countries with written constitutions, freedom of speech and of the press is not regarded as debarring the State from punishing or preventing abuse of this freedom.'[13]

Introduced on 10 May 1951, the first amendment was passed in little over a month of acrimonious debate in Parliament. The one significant concession Nehru allowed in a bid to douse the barrage of criticism coming his way was his acquiescence to the inclusion of the word 'reasonable' in the draft amendment. That of course meant that it could now be open to judicial interpretation whether restrictions that the government sought to impose on the right to freedom of speech passed the test of 'reasonableness'. However, dissenters remained unconvinced. As a *Times of India* editorial, entitled 'Not Enough', argued:

> Phrases such as 'reasonable restrictions', meant to be safeguards against the heavy hand of the government, can at best constitute only a partial check on the executive's abuse of powers. Experience shows that terms such as 'reasonable compensation' can carry a multitude of meanings. Moreover, those who may be victims of the new repressive laws are not always likely to have the means to seek legal redress. (Cited in Singh n. d.)

The final debate witnessed, according to a reporter for *The Times of India*, 'an intemperate and impassioned slanging match between the prime minister and Dr. Syama Prasad Mookerjee'. And so the first amendment was passed with a final count of 228 members in support of it, 20 opposed and around 50 abstaining. The indisputable fact is that the first amendment became law under an interim prime minister of a provisional government in a provisional parliament whose members were there by virtue of having been members of the Constituent Assembly. It was not until later in 1951—with the country's first general election beginning in 1950 and going well into the following year—that India got an elected government. Yet the arguments and counter-arguments these interim members raised were to surface in one form or the other in the years ahead. As for the Supreme Court, it endorsed the first amendment shortly after it became law in its 1951 verdict, *Shankari Prasad Singh Deo v. Union of India*. In 1957, *Virendra v. The State of Punjab and Another*, the Supreme Court, drawing from the first amendment, made the following observation:

> Our social interest ordinarily demands the free propagation and interchange of views but circumstances may arise when the social interest in public order may require a reasonable subordination of the social interest in free speech and expression to the needs of our social interest in public order. The Constitution recognises this necessity and has attempted to strike a balance between the two social interests. It permits the imposition of reasonable restrictions on the freedom of speech and expression in the interest of public order and on the freedom of carrying on trade or business in the interest of the general public.

The second major move by the government in its bid to control the press was to enact the Press (Objectionable Matter) Act of 1951, which was defined rather clumsily as 'an act to provide against the printing and publication of incitement to crime and other objectionable matter', and which came into force shortly after the first amendment had been passed. This law brought back many of the emergency powers that had been legislated by the colonial regime. It drew, for instance, from the powers granted by a law like the Indian Press (Emergency Powers) Act, 1931, which empowered provincial governments to demand a security deposit from presses which could then be forfeited if it published material that brought the government into disrepute. The Act defined 'objectionable matter' in the broadest possible terms, including 'words, signs or visible representation'. The fears and anxieties of the government of the day came through in its provisions, which included not just tensions over the government being overthrown or acts of sabotage and violence, but attempts to disrupt the supply and distribution of food and essential commodities. Also punishable was material deemed 'grossly indecent', 'scurrilous' or 'obscene'. The new law empowered the government to raid premises, seize and destroy unauthorised publications, seize and confiscate undeclared presses, and undertake other repressive measures. The very existence of this Act on the statute books appeared to undermine the foundation of Article 19(1)(a). Its saving grace was that it was meant to be a temporary law, unlike legislations like the 1931 Emergency Powers Act.

First Press Commission

Unsurprisingly, the country's first Press Commission, set up in 1952 under Justice G. S. Rajadhyakhsa, having studied the impacts of the Press (Objectionable Matters) Act of 1951, had no hesitation in calling for its repeal. It recorded 134 cases of publications being arraigned under its provisions—an overwhelming majority of which were lodged under Section 3(vi), applied to the rather loosely defined term 'scurrilous writing' (Muralidharan 2018: 129). This, the Commission went on to argue, was the exception rather than the rule, since a 'large section' of the Indian press was 'sober and responsible' and did not engage in 'yellow journalism'. Although it took another six years, the law was finally erased from the statue books after having been being amended a few times.

That First Press Commission, the third major move by the Nehruvian state to control the press, was mooted by Nehru during the first amendment debate in Parliament. Its aim—to 'examine the state of the Press and its contents'—was itself contentious and opposed by many newspaper proprietors of the time. Yet, looking back, there is some truth in media historian Krishna Ananth's observation that the Commission was ahead of its times, honing in as it did on '[a] host of issues concerned with the nexus between news and advertisements, the economics of the news industry and the impact of these on the role of the Press in the deepening of democracy or rendering the idea shallower …' (Ananth 2020a: 82). Many of the projections it made on how the media industry would shape up in the future proved prescient.

It is interesting to note that the Commission's definition of freedom of the press did not contradict the Supreme Court's conflation of press freedom and the constitutional guarantee of freedom of expression, despite Nehru's critical view of the judgment on *Romesh Thapar v. the State of Madras*, which had iterated that 'freedom of speech and expression includes freedom of propagation of ideas, and that freedom is ensured by the freedom of circulation'. The Commission, on its part, held that 'expression should be understood as meaning freedom to hold opinions, to receive and to impart information through the printed word, without interference from any public authority' (*Report of the Press Commission* 1954, part 1: 517). The 'tender plant of democracy', it stated, can only flourish in 'an atmosphere of the free interchange of views and ideas which one not only has a moral right but a moral duty to express'.

Unsurprisingly, the Commission's report, when it came out in 1954, two years after it was set up, raised the hackles of the big newspaper owners of the day. This was for two reasons. The first was its broad scope of inquiry, which ranged from tracing the growth of monopolies and the entry of big business into the industry to revisions in press laws. Second, the very pointed observations and recommendations it made had serious financial implications for the owners, who had cut many corners to run their establishments. The Commission, for instance, made no bones about its concern over the pressure brought to bear on the newspaper as a whole by the proprietor and senior staff, noting the 'extent to which external influences result in preventing the adequate and accurate presentation of news or the fair and adequate presentation of views which would serve to focus public opinion in the direction of social and general betterment' (*Report of the Press Commission* 1954, part 1: 313).

One of the Commission's major terms of reference was the conditions of work in the newspaper industry. It recognised the three kinds of employees that made up the industry: press workers, managerial staff and editorial staff. An entire chapter of its report was focused on the 'Working Journalist'. It found that most of the editorial staff was not given a contract or even a letter of appointment. Emoluments given were 'unsatisfactory' and there was no concept of a minimum wage. Sharp salary disparities between staffers of English-language newspapers and their Indian-language counterparts struck the Commission as patently unfair. It also pointed to the need to pay bonuses; draw up hours of work which should include a weekly rest, as well as holiday leave; timely promotions; retirement benefits; and gratuity.

Conspicuous among its recommendations, which would strike present-day employees as an incredulous position, was the right of employees to form unions. The Commission noted that in some newspaper establishments, attempts were made to dissuade working journalists from forming unions. This, the Commission sternly observed, was contrary to Article 19 of the Constitution. In fact, it paid a lot of attention to this issue, critiquing the commonly cited reasons for not unionising, including the facile argument that journalism is a profession entailing essentially 'brain work' and therefore does not lend itself to organisation along the lines of a trade union, for that would destroy the 'proper outlook of a true journalist, who considered his calling as a true mission'. This argument was dismissed out of hand by the Commission with the observation that the 'conduct of newspapers is no longer a mission, or even a profession; but has become an industry'. In fact, it argued, wage settlements for working journalists should rightfully come under the Industrial Disputes Act.

Commentators have noted that the Commission did not dwell too much on pressures on the press from the government. It however made careful note of pressures from advertisers, which it observed were reflected in 'unabashed puffs' making it into the editorial space. In Chapter 18, titled 'Bias & External Pressure', the Commission went hammer and tongs at the often unscrupulous ways in which advertisers try and influence news content: 'It has been suggested that the basis on which advertisers select their media will itself act as a source of pressure on newspaper'. It went on to observe that

> pressures from advertisers generally is [sic] applied to securing publication of laudatory material or suppression of unfavourable news. It is the practice of advertisers to issue to newspapers items of 'news' having the specific purpose of bringing before the eye of

the reader the name of the advertiser or of his products. (*Report of the Press Commission* 1954, part 1: 316)

The concern was expressed that powerful interests like advertisers would get the better of editors because 'there has been a general decline in the status and independence of the editor'.

The Commission also concluded that 'chain operations' in the industry only created an unequal playing field and argued that it would be best if every newspaper was seen as a separate unit so that profit and losses could be definitely ascertainable and competition made more 'even'.

Among the measures it suggested was the setting up of an All-India Press Council to maintain 'editorial independence, objectivity of news presentation and fairness of comment'; a Public Corporation to take over the PTI; and the enactment of statutes to define the powers, privileges and immunities of legislatures.

Taken together, these measures sought to broaden the ambit of what constitutes 'freedom of the press'. The threat to that freedom came from various quarters, ranging from vested interests which sought to control and influence news gathering to the lack of agency of journalists and their indifferent living standards.

Laws Brought in Following Commission's Recommendations

The government lost little time in legislating on the Commission's recommendations. In 1954, it enacted the Drugs and Magic Remedies (Objectionable Advertisements) Act. The next year saw the enactment of the Working Journalists and Other Newspaper Employees (Conditions of Service) and Miscellaneous Provisions Act, 1955, which sought to regulate the conditions of service of working journalists and newspaper employees. A year later came the Price-Page Schedule, which sought to check unequal access to resources among the various newspapers.

All three, of course, had raised the hackles of newspaper proprietors because they held grave implications for financial returns from their establishments.

The aim of the Drugs and Magic Remedies Act, as stated in the legislation, was to control and prohibit advertisements of 'certain drugs and remedies that claim to possess magic qualities to cure a disease or ailment'. The definition of what constitutes a 'magic remedy' was in itself an interesting comment on the efforts of the Nehruvian state to instil a 'scientific temper' in a population given to superstitions and irrational beliefs that were, in turn, exploited by charlatans and necromancers who often used the columns of newspapers to peddle their dubious, often dangerous, wares. The term 'magic remedy' has been defined under the Act to include 'a talisman, mantra, kavacha and any other charm of any kind which is alleged to possess miraculous powers or for affecting or influencing in any way the structure or any organic function of the body of human beings or animals'. Publication of any advertisement that promoted such spurious drugs and magic remedies was expressly and stringently prohibited. Interestingly, the Act also had an annexure listing 'disease, disorder or condition' that feed such advertising, including ubiquitous conditions such as cataracts, diabetes, sexual impotence and 'sterility in women'.

This meant, of course, that a pipeline of substantial earnings for newspaper establishments was blocked and contravening the provisions of the Act could potentially invite search and seizure operations and lengthy court cases.

Meanwhile the 'working journalist', popularised in the Commission's Report, emerged as a figure to defend and the welfare provisions extended to this category of professionals through the passage of the Working Journalists Act enjoyed considerable public support that went beyond the immediate stakeholders. Some commentators suggested that this was because memories of the much-lauded role of journalists in the freedom struggle were still fresh in the popular consciousness.

While presenting the Bill in Parliament, the Information Minister B. V. Keskar observed:

> In some ways, the Bill itself is not a major Bill. It is a small Bill ... But it is important ... that we are trying to apply it to an industry which up to this time was not able to get all these benefits, a piece of legislation, which, for the better working of our Press, for the better security of our journalists and therefore for a better, I would say, freedom of the press in this country ... (*Report of the Press Commission* 1954, Part 1: 382)

Others, like the left-leaning Hiren Mukherjee, elected to Parliament from the Calcutta North East constituency in the country's first general election, did not pull his punches while speaking against the power of newspapers owners in Parliament while the Bill was being discussed:

> The press has become a segment of big money, and that is why the right to start newspapers and rape the public mind is almost a fundamental right, which we cannot contest, of people who have been described by one of our leading journalists today as the Thugs and Pindaris of the press. It is against these Thugs and Pindaris of the press that the working journalist wants some sort of protection.

The lines of battle between the owners and their employers, drawn up in the report of the Commission, could not have been etched more sharply and the Working Journalists Act, 1955 in time came to be recognised as one of the most comprehensive pieces of protective legislation for journalists anywhere in the world. The Act tried to faithfully conform to the Press Commission's observations. It recognised the right of the Union Government to fix rates of wages in respect of both journalist and non-journalist employees and brought every newspaper establishment with more than 20 employees under the provisions of the Industrial Employment (Standing Orders) Act, 1946. The provisions of the Employees' Provident Funds Act, 1952, were similarly put in place until legislation specific to the sector was promulgated. The Union Government was also empowered to make rules on other sundry welfare measures, including payment of gratuity, stipulation of number of work hours and casual as well as earned leave. But what the proprietors perhaps came to regard as the most unkind cut of all was the stipulation that a Wage Board for fixing and revising rates of wages would be constituted from time to time by the Union Government.

Arguably the most radical piece of the three laws that were passed, the Price-Page Schedule, was introduced in 1956. It would seen by contemporary standards to 'distinctly smack of absurdity', as one commentator remarked (Muralidharan 2016: 270). But the Act drew on the Press Commission's conclusion that freedom of the press is considerably restricted by unequal access to resources among the various newspapers. It therefore sought to achieve parity between various players, rattling the proprietors of the bigger newspapers no end. The new law empowered the government to fix such schedules from time to time, which 'prescribed (a) the maximum number of pages that could be sold for the price, (b) the minimum number of pages that should be offered for the price, (c) the minimum of news and editorial matter that each issue must carry' (*Report of the Press Commission* 1954, Part 1: 465).

The preamble to the new law specifically referred to the Press Commission's recommendation and its emphasis on 'freedom of opinion' in the country:

The regulation of the prices of newspapers in relation to their sizes appeared to be a necessity to the Press Commission mainly in order to provide the circumstances in which freedom of opinion could be very much more real than it is today by eliminating unfair competition and equalising opportunities for newspapers especially for those with smaller resources.

The other stakeholder that the Commission had included in advocating a Price-Page Schedule was the reader: 'While on the question of the fair value given to the reader, we would like to record our opinion that the schedule should not … prescribe only the maximum number of pages that could be sold at a particular price, but also the minimum number that must be offered …We have stated elsewhere that in our view the quantum of advertisements in, say, a week's issue of a newspaper should not exceed 40 per cent of the total area and we feel this requirement should be made part of the schedule …' (Ananth 2020a: 87).

Unsurprisingly, when the Commission was trying to get a sense from the newspaper industry on its response to such a schedule, large newspaper establishments came out in bitter opposition to it while small newspapers endorsed it.

These recommendations only confirmed the worst fears of newspaper owners. Many proprietors had come out against the Nehru government when the first amendment was being considered. A 12-member delegation of the All India Newspaper Editors Conference (AINEC) had met Nehru on 20 May 1951, demanding that the government drop the proposed amendments or postpone it so that the response of the nation to it could be better assessed. Nehru on his part conveyed his commitment to the proposed changes while assuring the delegation that he would try and modify the amendments to address some of their concerns.

In fact Nehru did try to douse some of this resistance at that stage, and invited senior press personnel, like *Hindustan Times* editor Devdas Gandhi, proprietor of *The Indian Express* Ramnath Goenka and senior correspondent with *The Hindu*, Benegal Shiva Rao, to discuss the matter. Apparently such rearguard action proved ineffectual. Deshbandhu Gupta, an independent-minded member of the Congress who had spoken on press freedom during the Constituent Assembly debates, was among those who took issue with Nehru's approach. As Tripurdaman Singh reveals in *Sixteen Stormy Days: The Story of the First Amendment to the Constitution of India*, Gupta had in his private letters to Nehru argued that

> verbal assurances lacked any constitutional validity, and to give concrete form to them, suggested the inclusion of a new clause in the Constitution guaranteeing the freedom of the press—something akin to Article 1 of the American Constitution. 'These wide powers [which the government was appropriating via the amendment],' Gupta maintained, 'were an open invitation to parliamentary majorities to abridge the freedom of the press.' Nehru promptly rejected Gupta's suggestions out of hand.

When the Press Commission was set up in 1952, once again newspaper owners expressed their opposition to it, arguing that it would compromise their constitutional right of freedom of expression. 'While a body lobbying for the newspaper industry, the Indian and Eastern Newspaper Society (IENS), expressed consternation over the very setting up of such a commission, political supporters like C. Rajagopalachari, who was home minister at that point, argued that the 'legislation would only stifle freedom, when the press should be allowed space to work out its own regulatory modes through internal institutional mechanisms' (Muralidharan 2018: 270).

After the Press Commission's recommendations were implemented through legislation, newspaper owners approached the Supreme Court to have them struck down. The irony was that measures that were introduced by the Union Government to protect freedom of expression and press freedom were challenged by those opposing these laws on the very same basis: that they violated press freedom.

Notes

1. Jawaharlal Nehru in the Constituent Assembly, 13 December 1946. See Constituent Assembly Debates (1946).

2. K. T. Shah in the Constituent Assembly on 2 December 1948. See Constituent Assembly Debates (1948b).

3. Sardar Bhopinder Singh Man (Constituent Assembly Debates 1948b).

4. Shah, 1 December 1948 (Constituent Assembly Debates 1948a).

5. Damodar Swarup Seth (Constituent Assembly Debates 1948a).

6. Brajeshwar Prasad (Constituent Assembly Debates 1948b).

7. Shah (Constituent Assembly Debates 1948a).

8. Cited by Kazi Sued Karimuddin. See Constituent Assembly Debates (1948b).

9. See Tripurdaman Singh (n. d.), 'How the First Amendment to the Indian Constitution Circumscribed Our Freedoms & How it was Passed', excerpted from Singh's book *Sixteen Stormy Days: The Story of the First Amendment to the Constitution of India*.

10. See Parliamentary Debates (Government of India 1951). Retrieved from https://eparlib.nic.in/bitstream/123456789/760712/1/ppd_29-05-1951.pdf

11. Parliamentary Debates: Part II, p. 9082.

12. Parliamentary Debates: Part II, p. 9629.

13. A copy of the Act is available at https://legislative.gov.in/the-constitution-amendment-acts/ (accessed December 2024).

two

A Struggle without End for a Free Press

A good newspaper is a nation talking to itself.

This Arthur Miller quote draws from, and extends, an argument made by Harold Inis in his 1951 book, *The Bias of Communication*, where he observed that transformations of communication have shaped human history profoundly. Benedict Anderson recognised that 'print capitalism' helped to create the 'embryo of the nationally imagined community' (Anderson 1991: 44). Robin Jeffrey turned the focus onto India and the Indian newspaper scene in *India's Newspaper Revolution: Capitalism, Politics and the Indian-language Press 1977–99*. He pointed out that the newspaper in the country did two things: 'First, it made local language flourish … Second, newspapers created a daily ritual' that assured people 'that the imagined world is visibly rooted in everyday life' (Jeffrey 2000: 6).

One of the institutions that remained through the years of India's struggle for independence and which was seen as vital for the survival of the constitutional guarantee of freedom of speech and expression, and more expansively Indian democracy itself, was the newspaper. This was why there was such a flurry of press-related law-making and litigation around newspapers in the earliest days of the republic.

The Pre-Partition Scenario

Before revisiting some of those verdicts, it may be useful to gain an idea of the newspaper scene in the early twentieth century, before India gained independence. The years from the 1920s to the 1940s have been identified as a period of dynamic growth for Indian daily newspapers, given the churn created by the national movement and the emergence of an indigenous capitalist class in the country. Industrialists like G. D. Birla, Ramakrishna Dalmia and Ramnath Goenka, with their investments in jute, textiles, sugar, cement and paper, to name a few sectors they dominated, now began to demonstrate an active interest in running newspapers.

> For this class of 'absentee proprietors', the power and prestige attached to ownership or the possibility of using newspapers to further their business interests was more important than nurturing brilliant and independent journalism or even earning reasonable profits…. They signified the changeover from individual centred independent journalism of the earlier days to business centred modern journalism. (Nair 2003: 4182–4183)

There were several very talented editors nursing 'nationalist' newspapers across India like the *Free Press Journal*, *Sentinel*, *Hindustan Times* and *National Call*. The problem was that their establishments were poorly resourced and equipped, which left them out of the race against more privileged entities like *The Statesman*, well looked-after in those days with government advertising and more up-to-date technology. 'Having realised the significance of financial patronage, many newspapers were "flirting with" or trying to woo big businesses—to help the millowners in the name of "swadesh", boost Indian insurance in the name of nationalism, and support Indian shipping because it was a national enterprise' (Nair 2003: 4182).

According to one description provided in a court verdict,

> The newspaper industry in India did not originally start as an industry, but started as individual newspapers founded by leaders in the national, political, social and economic fields. During the last half a century, however, it developed characteristics of a profit making industry. Big industrialists investing money and controlling several newspapers all over the country became the special feature of this development.[1]

The fact that the majority of media owners were upper-caste, upper-class capitalists influenced the nature of the industry in more ways than one, and continues to do so right to the present day. It may account for one of major paradoxes that has marked the media—the lack of representation of important sections of the general population in the composition of the newsroom. Jeffrey was among the first to flag the reality that there are virtually no Dalits 'in editorial positions of any kinds, even though India's newspapers have grown spectacularly since the 1970s' (Jeffrey 2001: 225). Almost two decades later Sudipto Mondal reported that '[a]fter searching the country for more than 10 years, I have been able to find eight Dalit journalists in the English media' (Mondal 2017). Just to put this into perspective, according to the last census of 2011 there were over 200 million Dalits in the country.

First Press Commission

With independence, and at the goading of the Nehruvian State, the country got around to scrutinising more closely its newspaper scenario and the closest we can get, perhaps, to an accurate analysis of the actual state of newspapers in the immediate years after independence would be the First Press Commission Report which came out in 1954. For the first time, an attempt was made through this Commission to actually arrive at an estimate of the number of publications—both newspapers and periodicals—that were available to Indian readers at that juncture. According to the Report, there were 320 newspapers in English and major Indian languages, accounting for a circulation of 25.10 lakh. Minor languages accounted for a circulation of 0.15 lakh, and a solitary Chinese publication had a readership of 0.005 lakh (India's sole newspaper in Mandarin wound up in 2023!). What is interesting to note in the Press Commission's collation is that the English-language newspapers tended to have wider circulation. For instance, while there were 41 newspapers in the English language, together they accounted for 6.97 lakh readers. In contrast, while the Hindi language newspapers were far greater in number—76 to be precise—they accounted for only 3.79 lakh readers. All this, as we shall see, was to change drastically in the years ahead as emerging generations of Indians acquired literacy and an interest in reading newspapers. According to the Registrar of Newspapers for India (RNI), the number of dailies in the year 2021–2022 stood at 10,038, with Hindi dailies numbering 4,424 and claiming a circulation of 10.34 lakh, while English dailies stood at 825, with a claimed circulation of 2.09 lakh.

In the first three decades after independence, it was clearly the well-resourced English-language newspapers that dominated the scene. There were various reasons for this. The larger point regarding this state of affairs has been made by Ghalib scholar Hasan Abdullah, who argues that the Indian intelligentsia had adopted English as its virtual mother tongue and had been largely unconcerned about their respective mother tongues. He notes, 'I have been associated with an Urdu monthly that regularly carries sections on societal affairs, economics, international affairs, and science, besides literature; the experience suggests that[,] leave alone getting original articles, even to get good translations of serious articles is a very difficult proposition' (Abdullah 2006: 226). Rare are the instances, he points out, of intellectuals like astrophysicist J. V. Narlikar, who made it a point to write on science in Marathi.

The First Press Commission report provided a structural reason for this preponderance of the English language: 'The availability of capital and the existence of potential readership, i.e., literacy combined with purchasing power are important factors that determine the centres of newspaper production ...' (*Report of the Press Commission* 1954, part 1: 18). Daily newspapers, it found, were confined largely to metropolitan cites and larger capitals, and their great advantage was that the metropolitan press tended to entice journalistic talent that might have otherwise gone to the development of a local press.

As we saw in Chapter 1, it was the first time in India that a government-appointed panel like the First Press Commission sought to define the first principles for the functioning of an independent press. It had a raft of objectives, and first on the list was safeguarding the freedom of the press and helping the institution maintain its independence. Following from this was the need to censure objectionable types of journalistic conduct, by both practitioners and proprietors, and build codes of functioning that would conform to the highest professional standards. To achieve such an outcome, the Commission added more stipulations, including regulations against monopolies and the regular monitoring of the performance of the press across the country. It recommended that the Registrar of Newspapers maintain detailed information on publications that are mandatorily registered with them and that a Press Council be established to address ongoing issues in the sector.

It also expended considerable space and energy to highlighting the need for good editors:

> We consider it essential that if a newspaper is to fulfill its function in society, it should have a certain unity of purpose which could only be possible if the concentration of ultimate responsibility resides in one person ... and where all members of the editorial staff realize that they are working towards a common goal under the leadership of the editor.... This requires an individual who can inspire all members of the team with their journalistic abilities as well as absolute integrity. (*Report of the Press Commission* 1954, part 1: 333)

The Commission saw the future of the Press as hinged closely to the independence of the editor and recommended that the period of notice for an editor should not be less than three months during the first three years of service, and not less than six months thereafter.

Unsurprisingly, newspaper proprietors of the day were not keen to have the First Press Commission inquire into their affairs, a move they saw as unduly intrusive. Resistance to the whole process became clear from the very beginning, when the Commission began seeking information from them. Some 18,000 copies of a statement eliciting facts of the establishment on issues like circulation had been dispatched to the owners of 7,335 newspapers and periodicals. Replies were received from just 100 of them! The First Press Commission adopted both conciliatory measures, such as asking for briefer particulars, as well as tougher ones like issuing show cause notices to prise open this black box of information. It was only partly successful—many proprietors continued to steadfastly ignore requests, reminders, show cause notices, and even summons for personal appearances, as the Press Commission was to later note regretfully.

Among newspaper owners who freely and publicly expressed their reservations against the First Press Commission was Ramnath Goenka, proprietor of the *Express* group. It is said that when 'Lala' Sri Ram asked him about rumours that the *Express* might close, he replied that this could happen 'in case the Government is foolish enough to accept the recommendations of the Press Commission … where nobody who knew anything about the economy of newspaper production was there' (cited in Verghese 2005: 93).

Goenka's was a jaundiced view of a proprietor anxious to protect his interests, especially his pecuniary interests. As a media academic observed,

> For owners of the press, freedom meant a quite literal interpretation of laissez faire when they would be answerable only to the market, the profit calculus, and their own sense of responsibility towards a newly independent nation. For journalists and their unions, freedom meant liberation from the tyranny of their owners' rather skewed understanding of what constituted news and public interest. (Muralidharan 2018: 266)

This tension between the two sides became more manifest after the First Press Commission Report came out. By diagnosing certain endemic problems that stymied the sector and suggesting ameliorative measures, it may even be argued that the Commission was doing the industry—and by extension the proprietors—a favour. But that was not how it was perceived by those who controlled the industry.

Working Conditions of Journalists

There was, for instance, a lack of standardisation that had beset the sector, including what the Commission saw as a 'bewildering variety of staff doing different kinds of work'. It was pointed out that the capitalist instinct of owners was to plough back profits into existing concerns and explore possibilities of starting new ones, rather than trying to improve the working conditions of journalists. Through their extractive model of functioning, the newspapers of post-independence India provided a snapshot of the growth and evolution of Indian capitalism (Jeffrey 1994).

While proprietors were in denial about these abysmal working conditions, senior professionals from within the journalistic community began to take a greater initiative in documenting their realities. One such individual was J. P. Chaturvedi, who was appointed as a member of the inquiry commission to examine the condition of Hindi journalists, and later an inquiry conducted by the All-India Hindi Patrakar Sangh. In his memoirs, published in 1992, he recalled being brought in direct touch with the pitiable working conditions of the working journalist and how jokes were made about who is a 'working' journalist and who is a 'non-working journalist'. An all-India convention of journalists was held in Delhi in October 1950 after which the decision was taken to set up the Indian Federation of Working Journalists. Chaturvedi's home became the headquarters of this body. It was from here that the publication *Working Journalist* was also brought out.

Chaturvedi pointed out how the First Press Commission, because it thought the profession served as an essential adjunct to democracy and must be staffed by people of high calibre, had recommended a remuneration of Rs 225 for journalists working in the cities of Bombay, Calcutta, Delhi and Madras, and Rs 150 elsewhere in India, and how even these modest sums were not acceptable to the proprietors. It was in that context that the Statutory Wage Board was envisaged to fix fair rates of wages for all categories of working journalists.

The move to protect security of service was seen as the biggest guarantor of independent journalism at a point when feudal norms of work were still largely prevalent. The Working Journalists (Conditions of Service) and Miscellaneous Provisions Act, enacted in 1955, was an extremely important step towards the protection of journalists from arbitrary dismissal without due notice of three months in the case of working journalists and six months in the case of editors. It also laid down that no employee in a newspaper establishment shall be dismissed by an employer because of any liabilities they may have incurred after following government-specified rates of payment.

More provisions to protect security of service were introduced through rules which came three years later, mandating that when a working journalist's services are terminated for any reason, other than as punishment inflicted by way of disciplinary action, he or she is entitled to cash compensation for earned leave not availed of up to a maximum of 90 days. In addition, Section 8 of the Act mandated the creation of a Wage Board for fixing rates of wages for working journalists from time to time. R. Venkataraman, who was to later become India's president, revealed the parliamentary push given to this process: 'It was my pleasure and privilege, as a Member of the First Lok Sabha, to take up certain issues pertaining to the welfare of working journalists. The application of the Industrial Disputes Act to journalists was being actively discussed in the Parliament at that time' (Chaturvedi 1992). Later Venkataraman represented journalists in the First Wage Board and observed, 'In seeking protection for working journalists we were, in effect, trying to obtain legislative sanction for an important historical process' (ibid.).

Since the first Wage Board was constituted in 1956, there have been five others. Their awards have invariably been met with dogged resistance from newspaper proprietors. The last one, set up under Justice Majithia in 2007, for instance, gave its award in December 2010, and it was immediately challenged in the Supreme

Court. In 2014, the apex court found nothing objectionable about it, much to the angst of the employers. Initially the Wage Board existed only for journalists. This was changed when the Act was amended in 1974 and provision was made for an additional wage board for non-journalist employees of newspapers.

The connection between the well-being of journalists and the flourishing of democracy and citizens' rights was well recognised by the Supreme Court. In its 1959 verdict, *Express Newspapers (Pvt) Ltd. v. Union of India,* the Court stated, 'Working journalists are but the vocal organs and the necessary agencies for the exercise of the right of free speech and expression....'

Proprietors Go to Court

Tensions between the newspaper industry and the government over the rights of journalists and the exercise of freedom of speech and expression that had been building up through the early 1950s deepened, as we saw, when the Nehruvian government undertook to legislate on some of the Commission's recommendations. This resulted in proprietors taking recourse to the courts. The faultlines were to emerge very clearly in three major cases: *Express Newspapers (Pvt) Ltd. v. Union of India, 1959*; *Sakal Papers (P) Ltd., and Others v. Union of India, 1961* and *Bennett Coleman v. Union of India, 1972.*

It is useful to recall the backdrop against which *Express Newspapers (Pvt) Ltd. v. Union of India* was heard. When the first Wage Board came up with its award, *The Indian Express* under its proprietor Ramnath Goenka, an uncompromising critic of the reforms suggested by the First Press Commission, along with several other newspaper establishments and the existing news agency, Press Trust of India, challenged it before the Supreme Court.

The final verdict provided an interesting snapshot of what was at stake for Goenka. Express Newspapers (Private) Ltd. was the biggest chain in the newspaper world in the country and published *Indian Express*, an English daily, from Madras, Bombay, Delhi and Madurai; a weekly in English, the *Sunday Standard*, from Madras, Bombay and Delhi; a Tamil daily, *Dinmani,* from Madras and Madurai; and a Tamil weekly, *Dinmani Kadir*, from Madras. Besides that it owned a Marathi daily, *Lokasatta*, and Marathi weekly, *Sunday Lokasatta*, both published from Bombay; *Screen*, an English weekly from Bombay; and *Andhra Prabha*, a Telugu daily and weekly. Working journalists employed by the group numbered 331 and their total emoluments amounted to Rs 977,892. If the Wage Board decision came into effect, this figure would rise to Rs 1,521,282.12.[2]

The petitioners contended that the Act had 'violated their fundamental rights under Arts. 19(1)(a), 19(1)(g), 14 and 32 of the Constitution'. Further, that the Wage Board award had been arrived at 'without any consideration whatsoever as to the capacity of the newspaper industry to pay the same, imposed too heavy a financial burden on the industry and spelled its total ruin'. It was pointed out that Section 9(1) of the Working Journalists Act (WJA) 'made it incumbent on the Wage Board to take into consideration the capacity of the newspaper industry to pay the rates and scales of wages recommended by it'. Since it had not done so, the petition argued, the Wage Board's decision should be held void.

Interestingly, it brought in Article 19(1)(a) into its argument, maintaining that the Working Journalists Act, by authorising the fixation of salaries of working journalists, would end up disabling the running of the press and thus infringing the right to freedom of expression.

The Government of India, which was the first respondent in the case, gave a spirited reply. It also recognised that the work of a journalist is unique and demands a high degree of general education and some kind of specialised training.... The working journalists are a class by themselves apart from the other employees of the newspaper establishments and also employees in other industries. They can be singled out for the purpose of ameliorating their conditions of service. There would be no discrimination if special legislation is enacted for the benefit of this class and a special machinery is created for fixing the rates of its wages different from the machinery for other workmen.

The courts interestingly pushed back against what was perceived as the threat of State control of the media. The Wage Board's award was held to be ultra vires by the Supreme Court in early 1958, chiefly because the court held that the Wage Board had not considered sufficiently the capacity of the newspaper industry to pay wages at the rates fixed by it. The central government responded swiftly to this development by promulgating, in June 1958, an ordinance called the Working Journalists (Fixation of Rates of Wages) Ordinance, replacing it with an Act with the same name in September 1958 (*Report of the Working Journalists Wage Committee*: 4). This time, care was taken to scrutinise the financials of a cross-section of newspapers, after which the Committee came to the conclusion that the newspaper industry as a whole had a stable future in the country. It made a raft of recommendations, including classifications of areas of operation and categorisations of employees from the editor to the proofreader (ibid.: 15). In 1974, the Act was amended to constitute two statutory Wage Boards—one for working journalists and the other for non-journalist newspaper employees.

Managements of the big newspapers—which were earlier reluctant to provide information about their finances to institutions like the First Press Commission, seemed more than anxious to use the argument that had worked in their favour in

Express Newspapers (Pvt) Ltd. v. Union of India to render laws based on some of the Press Commission's recommendations ultra vires. They sensed that the Supreme Court was open to viewing the press as an industry rather than as a 'public utility' for civil society participation in the way the Press Commission had envisaged it. As a media academic put it, 'Successive judicial rulings, tended both to narrow the amplitude of the free speech right and make newspaper owners the privileged repository of that entitlement, and also spare them any obligation of financial disclosure' (Muralidharan 2018: 388).

To understand the second case that was flagged, *Sakal Papers v. Union of India, 1961*, we need to reference major reforms suggested by the Press Commission to try and create a level playing field for all newspapers. The Commission had found that out of a total of 330 dailies existing at that time, five owners controlled 29 newspapers and 31.2 per cent of the circulation, indicating what it termed as a 'considerable degree of concentration' which it declared was 'not desirable in the interest of freedom of choice' (*Report of the Press Commission* 1954, part 1: 501). It therefore suggested a mechanism that would fix a minimum price at which papers of a particular size can be sold and laid down the quantum of advertising that can be allowed. This Price-Page Schedule recommendation led to a sharp polarisation among newspaper proprietors. While the big newspaper houses were bitterly opposed to the idea, smaller establishments enthusiastically endorsed the idea. In 1956, the Government of India passed The Newspaper (Price and Page) Act based on this recommendation, followed four years later by the Daily Newspaper (Price and Page) Order, 1960.

It was to strike down both the Act and the order that the large Marathi language newspaper group, Sakal, went to the Supreme Court claiming that they were in contravention of Article 19(1)(a) of the Constitution and did not conform to any of the exceptions cited in Article 19(2). Sakal claimed a circulation in Maharashtra and Karnataka of 52,000 copies on weekdays and 56,000 copies on Sundays. It argued that a citizen had the right to propagate their ideas, disseminate them and circulate them and that right extended not merely to the 'matter' that was circulated but also the 'volume of circulation'. By restraining the latter, it was interfering with freedom of speech and expression. It also stated that 'freedom of speech could not be restricted for the purpose of regulating the commercial aspect of the activities of newspapers'.[3] Under the Order they would have to either increase their cover price, which would affect their circulation, or reduce the number of pages of the newspapers, thereby undermining their right to freedom of expression.

Among the counter-arguments raised by the defendant, the Government of India, was the argument that both the Act and the order would enable newspapers in general to exercise their rights of freedom of speech and expression. Besides, the reason *Sakal* was able to increase its pages was that it devoted a larger volume of space to advertisements. This could not be seen as 'the lawful exercise of their right of freedom of speech and expression or of the right of dissemination of news and views'.[4]

The apex court, however, saw virtue in the petitioners' arguments. It set aside the Act as unconstitutional, with the order being rendered null and void as a consequence. The court observed,

> The advertisement revenue of a newspaper is proportionate to its circulation. Thus the higher the circulation of a newspaper the larger would be its advertisement revenue. So if a newspaper with a high circulation were to raise its price its circulation would go down and this in turn would bring down also the advertisement revenue. That would force the newspaper either to close down or to raise its price. Raising the price further would affect the circulation still more and thus a vicious cycle would set in which

would ultimately end in the closure of the newspaper. If, on the other hand, the space for advertisement is reduced the earnings of a newspaper would go down and it would either have to run at a loss or close down or raise its price. The object of the Act in regulating the space for advertisements is stated to be to prevent 'unfair' competition. It is thus directed against circulation of a newspaper. When a law is intended to bring about this result there would be a direct interference with the right of freedom of speech and expression guaranteed under Article 19(1)(a).

Media scholars have over the years debated this verdict and many have come to the conclusion that it did not secure Article 19(1)(a), as the judges had argued, but in fact had the opposite effect. This view relied on a more holistic reading of the issue, to include the diversity of sources from which information is disseminated in the media. Concentration of media ownership, which the Act was attempting to prevent, 'also implies reduction in diversity of sources ... which consequently become[s] one factor of many which touches upon the reduction in diversity of opinions in the media' (Kumar 2016). Building an environment that allows smaller newspapers with diverse and varying viewpoints would in fact amount not to a 'violation of free speech by the government, but to a fulfillment of its obligation to ensure the freedom of speech' (Bhatia 2016: 23).

The third important judgment, which came almost a decade later, *Bennett Coleman v. Union of India, 1972*, drew greatly from the verdicts that had given relief to newspaper proprietors—*Express Newspapers* and, more specifically, *Sakal Papers*. This petition challenged the newsprint control policy of the Government of India, introduced earlier that year. Scarcity of newsprint was a recurrent problem and State efforts to regulate access to it had often led to friction, even before independence. The petitioners in the 1972 case argued that the newsprint control policy violated their right to free speech and expression, since it authorised a 20 per cent increase in newsprint allocation only for newspapers of less than 10 pages. This amounted to discrimination against newspapers that had more than 10 pages, which as it happened also infringed upon the equality guarantee (Article 14) based on no 'reasonable classification'. This amounted to 'newspaper control'.

The freedom of speech and expression argument was used extensively by the petitioners:

> The liberty of the press remains an Ark of the Covenant. The newspapers give the people the freedom to find out which ideas are correct. Therefore the freedom of the press is to be enriched by removing the restrictions on page limit and allowing them to have new editions of newspapers.[5]

They argued that if, on the one hand, as a result of page reduction, newspapers came to depend on advertisement as their main source of income, it would deprive them of their freedom of speech and expression. On the other hand, if as a result of a restriction on the number of pages newspapers were forced to sacrifice advertisements, they could be badly hit financially. This could lead to the closing down of operations, which again would mean an infringement on their freedom of speech and expression.

Four judges of the five-judge bench were persuaded by these arguments and struck down the newspaper control policy for violating both Article 14 and Article 19(1)(a), because it sought to limit a paper's size, readership and growth and did not constitute a reasonable restriction under 19(2). It validated the petitioners' argument that 'the policy of the Government to limit all papers at 10 pages is arbitrary. It tends to treat unequals as equals and discriminates against those who by virtue of their efficiency, standard and service and because of their All-India stature acquired a higher page level in 1957.'[6] It also noted sympathetically that since advertisements were the main source of income for these entities, the loss of revenue they would have to incur, running into several lakhs, would be very destabilising for their operations.

The fifth judge dissented and upheld the newsprint policy. He argued that freedom of expression is not only an individual good, but a social good.

> With the concentration of mass media in a few hands, the chance of an idea antagonistic to the idea of the proprietors of the big newspapers getting access to the market has become very remote. It is no use having a right to express your idea, unless you have got a medium for expressing it. The concept of a free market for ideas presupposes that every type of idea will get into the market and if free access to the market is denied for any ideas, to that extent, the process of competition becomes limited and the chance of all the ideas coming to the market is removed.

As things stood, he observed, the 'modern big paper' had the greatest chance of getting itself known to the public. This also affected the economic pattern of society: 'Whether or not the modern big newspaper is the cultural arm of the industry, it has an interest in the present method of production and distribution, as it subsists mainly upon advertisement'. He then went on to cite the 1969 report of the Mahalanobis Committee on Distribution of Income and Levels of Living, which highlighted the inter-linkages between newspapers and big business in the country. The problem, the dissenting judge asked, is how all ideas were to be brought into the market, so that the concept of freedom of speech was a live one? He wrote, 'The freedom of speech, if it has to fulfil its historic mission, namely, the spreading of political truth and the widest dissemination of news, must be a freedom for all citizens in the country'. This led him to conclude that 'a scheme for distribution of a commodity like newsprint which will subserve the purpose of free flow of ideas to the market from as many different sources as possible would be a step to advance and enrich that freedom'.[7]

The dissenting judgment, in other words, as a legal scholar has pointed out, made a 'distinction between abridging speech, and abridging the freedom of speech … the newsprint quota did abridge speech (in the crude, factual sense that if you had less newsprint, you can "speak" less), but not the freedom of speech' (Bhatia 2016: 293). He also noted that this dissenting opinion proved a 'rich and complex substantive vision underlying Article 19(1)(a) … First, free speech guarantees the right of the individual person to express herself. Second, it is also the right of the community to hear and to be informed. And third, it is a social good, contributing to a thriving democratic community' (ibid.: 296–297).

Battle for Newsprint

Newsprint, as the most important raw material in the production of a newspaper and accounting for at least half its production costs, remained a contentious issue between the State and newspaper proprietors. Scarcity of newsprint was constantly raising its head. In the 1950s, the Korean war had led to supplies sharply declining and the government introducing import licences for newsprint. Over the years, regulatory authorities were set up and attempts were made to limit the number of pages a newspaper could carry.

The petitioners in the 1984 case, *Indian Express Newspapers (Bombay) Private Ltd and Ors v. Union of India and Ors*, argued that import duty for newsprint, introduced in 1982, had the 'direct effect of crippling the freedom of speech and expression guaranteed by the Constitution as it led to the increase in the price of newspapers and the inevitable consequence of reduction of their circulation.'[8] They also found irrational the classification of newspapers into big, medium and small. This allowed total exemption from such duties to those with a circulation less than 15,000; only 5 per cent ad valorem duty to those with a circulation between 15,000 and 50,000; while newspapers with a circulation of over 50,000 were forced to pay 15 per cent ad valorem duty, which worked out to Rs 825 per metric tonne.

The court agreed that '[f]reedom of [the] press ... means freedom from interference from authority which would have the effect of interference with the content and circulation of newspapers.' But it found no fault in the classification of newspapers made for the purpose of exception of duties: 'We do not find anything sinister in the object nor can it be said that the classification has no nexus with the object to be achieved' (that is, creating a level playing field for small- and medium-sized newspapers). The court, however, did order the Government of India to 'reconsider within six months the entire question of levy of import duty or auxiliary duty payable by the petitioners and others on newsprint used for printing newspapers, periodicals etc. with effect from March 1, 1981'.

The Second Press Commission, set up in 1982, also attempted to answer the vexed question of how to ensure a level playing field when it came to managing newsprint. It pointed out that with the liberalised policy of import and distribution of newsprint from March 1977, big newspapers had increased their pages substantially and therefore recommended that 'newspapers should be allowed newsprint free of import/excise duties up to the level of 12 pages' (*Report of the Second Press Commission* 1982, vol. 1: 128).

This was a time, from the 1960s to the 1980s, when newspapers had acquired the contours of a rapidly expanding business—even while propagating the belief that their business was all about expanding the citizens' right to freedom of expression, as their many plaints in court would indicate.

Commercialisation of the Newspaper

It is said that when Ramkrishna Dalmia, one of the country's largest industrialists, acquired *The Times of India* from Bennett Coleman and Co. in 1946, it signaled that 'a learned profession' was becoming 'a commercial business' (Nair 2003). But perhaps nothing indicated the growing commercialisation of the press more clearly than the institutionalisation of the Audit Bureau of Circulation (ABC), set up in 1948, which was seen as a 'landmark in the history of Indian capitalism and consumerism' (Jeffrey 1994) since it provided a mechanism for commercial interests to hone in on publications that would best advertise their products. Twice a year the ABC published its compilation of the names and circulations of newspapers and magazines that were its clients. This information expedited commerce in unprecedented ways as potential advertisers could now see how many newspapers were being sold and where they were being sold in order to arrive at informed decisions on their ad placements.

Another significant institution related to the newspaper industry came up a decade later. On the recommendation of the Press Commission, the Registrar of Newspapers was instituted in 1956. Every new publication was required to register itself with this body, which existed not just to receive such applications but to ensure that there were no duplicate titles, to check the veracity of circulation figures and to record statements that publications had to come up with every year. It also came up with an annual report. This became a regulatory mechanism when an amendment was made to the Press and Registration of Books Act of 1867, and the passing of the Registration of Newspapers (Central) Rules, 1956.

Both institutions, in their distinct ways, helped the press expand in commercial terms—a process that was assisted greatly by the National Readership Survey, a tool created by stakeholders in the advertising sector to help gain better insights into the newspaper market. As Jeffrey (1994) observed, the four National Readership Surveys (the first of which came out in 1970), were 'unabashedly geared to competitive selling, using techniques of international capitalism.... Each can be seen as a milestone in the survival and expansion of Indian consumer capitalism as it began to face a less and less hostile state' (1994: 756). Interestingly, both the newspaper and the advertising sector, he pointed out, made use of these market surveys to try and break out of the structures created in the 1950s and 1960s by a State striving for 'socialism'.

Controlling the Media Narrative

There were also attempts by non-State actors to control the media narrative. A striking example of this was when the Panthic Committee, during the years of militancy in Punjab, decreed that the press and government-run electronic media desist from using the word 'terrorist' to characterise their followers. To ensure that this injunction was taken seriously, the station director of All India Radio (AIR) in Chandigarh was gunned down (*India Today* 1990).

Ironically enough, from the 1960 to the 1980s, the Indian State—while not quite ready to embrace the markets fully—was losing its appetite to ensure a level playing field between big newspaper concerns and the smaller players in the market, even as its espousal of the 'socialism model' of the Nehruvian years steadily declined. This, along with court judgments that favoured big newspapers, allowed newspaper monopolies to flourish. The data bear this out: there were only two dailies in 1960 with a circulation of one lakh and above and both were English-language publications. By 1979, there were 30 of them, with 20 in Indian languages (*Report of the Second Press Commission* 1982).

The Indian State also felt the need to control dissent and by extension press freedoms. In 1957 we had *Virendra v. State of Punjab*, which laid down that the free speech guarantee could be overruled to ensure public order. Five years later, the Supreme Court in its judgment, *Kedar Nath Singh v. State of Bihar, 1961*, ensured that sedition stayed in the statute books, despite the Constituent Assembly debates that had outlawed it. The court did, however, make it clear that the application of the law was limited to 'acts involving intention or tendency to create disorder, or disturbance of law and order, or incitement to violence'.

There was a conspicuous tightening of the state's coercive apparatus following the 1962 war with China. Nehru's government amended the Constitution for the sixteenth time in January 1963. Article 19(2) now included what amounted to another limitation on the freedom of speech and expression, with the Union government empowered to undertake any measure necessary to preserve and maintain the integrity and sovereignty of the country. This amendment enabled the enactment of the draconian Unlawful Activities (Prevention) Act (UAPA) in 1967.

Other legislative actions have granted the State more room for arbitrary actions against dissent, with direct implications for the media. The Terrorist and Disruptive Activities (Prevention) Act (TADA), 1987, outlawed any act of speech 'through any media' which 'questions, disrupts or is intended to disrupt, whether directly or indirectly, the sovereignty and territorial integrity of India'. The 2002 Prevention of Terrorism Act (POTA), like TADA, stripped journalists of the right to protect their sources. While both TADA and POTA were subsequently withdrawn, many of their brutal provisions were incorporated in the UAPA, which went on to be amended six times. The question is whether these laws have given the Indian State far greater presumptive powers than envisaged in the Constitution. From all the evidence, they seem to have given the State the upper hand when it comes to interpretive disputes (Khosla 2012: 137).

The Emergency

While journalists, including editors, suffered a great deal as a result of these draconian laws, it is during the Emergency (1975–1977) that we saw the might of the State pitted against the institution of the press and individual journalists in a more direct way. It may be worthwhile in a work that looks at the media's right to free speech and expression to consider this interregnum more closely.

What is striking is that, just a year before the proclamation of the Emergency, the Supreme Court had recognised the right to dissent and observed, 'Peaceful protests and the voicing of a contrary opinion are powerful, wholesome weapons in the democratic repertoire.'[9]

That, however, did not dissuade Prime Minister Indira Gandhi from declaring—on 26 June 1975—the Emergency on the grounds that the country faced imminent internal and external threats to its security. While those were the ostensible reasons, the proximate one was that she feared for her own political future. Early that June, the Allahabad High Court had passed a judgment holding her guilty of electoral malpractices, and disqualifying her from holding public office for six years. When the matter was taken up to the Supreme Court, it granted only a partial stay to that judgment, much to her dissatisfaction.

The proclamation of the Emergency was accompanied by widespread arrests of politicians and political leaders across the country under the Maintenance of Internal Security Act (MISA), 1971. A Censorship Order was also issued under the Defence of India Rules, 1971, on the same day, which laid down that no news, comment, rumour or report relating to any action taken under certain provisions of either the Defence of India Rules or MISA could be published unless it was previously submitted to the appointed censor ('authorised officer'). This was accompanied by executive guidelines, among which was the line: 'Nothing is to be published that is likely to convey the impression of a protest or disapproval of a governmental measure.'

In the initial days there was some semblance of opposition, like spaces for editorials left blank and the like. But these came to be very rare and, in time, given the threats issued by officialdom, most publications fell in line, with even the occasional satirical cartoon falling out of view, as also the popular *Shankar's Weekly*, which shut down permanently two weeks after the Emergency was declared. Some other publications, notably *Hindustan Times*, tilted in the other direction by demonstrating an unabashed support for the government, while *The Times of India* also soon surrendered its independence given that one-third of its board of directors were government nominees.

Those newspapers that did not toe the government line were made to face consequences. A proposal was made to the proprietor of *The Indian Express* (IE), R. P. Goenka, that he sell his newspaper chain to the Congress or its nominees. When Goenka refused, 'the government decided to use strong-arm tactics' (Kapoor 2015: 155). The pressures brought on him included investigation into its finances and punitive taxation.

> On August 18, 1976, a drastic individual precensorship order was specifically imposed on the *Indian Express*. The IE challenged this action in the State High Court of Bombay. After a few days the precensorship order was unconditionally withdrawn.... Next month the electric supply to its press in Delhi was cut off for alleged arrears of electricity due.... As a result of another writ

petition, a mandatory order was passed by the Delhi High Court and the supply was restored. (Sorabjee 1977: 18)

Following this, the press was sealed, but once again the court ordered the seal to be removed. The newspaper was also denied banking credit facilities.

Within weeks of the Emergency being declared, several foreign correspondents were expelled from the country and Kuldip Nayar, a senior editor with *IE*, was arrested (Borders 1975). *The Statesman* had its government advertisements suspended, and the threat of arrest hovered over its editor during those 21 months. Through it all, AIR and Doordarshan, as also the official news agency Samachar, projected the government's actions in a positive light. A notice was issued in December 1975 under the Companies Act proposing the appointment of an unspecified number of government directors on *The Statesman*'s board. Hearings before the Calcutta High Court carried on, but the government a year later unilaterally withdrew the notice. However, its managing director was indicted before a magistrate's court on the charge of having acquired a small publishing company for The Statesman Ltd in 1970 without seeking the necessary government approval. His passport was also impounded without any reasons being cited.

Such actions, designed to disrupt the functioning of independent newspapers, continued throughout the Emergency. These included secret instructions to public sector companies not to advertise in these publications. Nothing reflected the steady strangulation of constitutional guarantees that marked the era as much as the *ADM Jabalpur v. Shivkant Shukla* judgment delivered in April 1976, which argued that under an Emergency a citizen's constitutional guarantees would stand suspended.

A particularly significant development in terms of press freedom was the enactment of the Prevention of Publication of Objectionable Matter Act, 1976. An Act under the same name, enacted in 1951, had been repealed in 1957 on the grounds that it was destructive of press freedoms. This version was even worse. It had an express provision for preventive action against newspapers, making it possible to prohibit the publication of a newspaper for a period not exceeding two months. Even the courts could not intervene against such preventive orders.

This law was one of a trio of laws passed in February 1976 by the Indira Gandhi government that media scholar V. Krishna Ananth (2020b) termed as 'legal (but illegitimate) measures' against media freedoms. The other two were the Parliamentary Proceedings (Protection of Publication) Repeal Act, 1976, and the Press Council (Repeal) Act, 1976. Together they replaced ordinances passed a few months earlier. Speaking in the Rajya Sabha in January 1976, Mrs Gandhi pulled no punches while arguing in favour of censorship:

> It is obvious that the opposition movement was not merely getting publicity, but was actually built up by our press; and it is because we denied the opposition the benefit of this, their special type of publicity, that the emergency has succeeded. In a battle the antagonists' lines of supply have to be cut off, and this is what censorship has done. (Kapoor 2015: 63)

When the Emergency came to an end in 1977, it unleashed, according to one assessment, three phenomena: 'curiosity, capitalism and technology blended to propel the advertising industry and the expansion of all forms of media' (Jeffrey 2000: 65).

When the Janata Party came to power after the General Election of 1977, the three laws were repealed, which in effect meant that not only were the draconian features of the first nullified, but the Parliamentary Proceedings (Protection of Publication) Act of 1956 guaranteeing the right of the press to report on parliamentary proceedings without fear of defamation was once again the law, and the Press Council was revived as an institution. While in a formal sense the laws were withdrawn, many of the methodologies of control that were refined during this period, including censorship, suspension of the capacity to publish, and the strategic deployment of advertising support, have haunted the media ever since and continue to do so to the present day. Decades later, most conspicuously under the BJP-led Union government since 2014, journalists have had to spend long years in jail after anti-terror laws like the UAPA and the sedition law were used against them.

The Second Press Commission

The Janata Party also set up the Second Press Commission in May 1978. However, by the time the final report emerged in 1982, Indira Gandhi was back in power. Its chair, Justice P. C. Goswami, had no alternative but to resign. The new chair, Justice K. K. Mathew, introduced a distinctive note of pragmatism which made its way into the final report.

The newspaper scene had changed considerably since the days of the First Press Commission. The exponential growth in the number of publications was now conspicuous, with the country having the fourth largest number of newspapers in the world. The urban-centric nature of this growth was patent now, with the bigger cities accounting for 93.3 per cent of total circulation. But there was one major difference: Indian-language newspapers were growing at a much faster rate of growth than English-language ones. English had yielded its top position to Hindi. As media commentator Sevanti Ninan notes, '*The Times of India*, claiming to be the world's largest circulated broadsheet in the English language, ranked at No 11 in the NRS [National Readership Survey] of 2006. Hindi newspapers occupied three of the top five positions' (Ninan 2007: 16). *Eenadu* (Telugu) and *Lokmat* (Marathi) were the others in the top five. Others like *Daily Thanthi* (Tamil) and *Malayala Manorama* (Malayalam) followed closely. Robin Jeffrey uncovered important reasons for regional-language dailies flourishing at this juncture.

> The surge in circulation, provoked by *Eenadu*'s extraordinary commitment to local coverage and distribution, plus fierce competition from a new rival, improved the penetration of Telugu dailies from something like ten per 1,000 people in 1991 to 20 per 1,000 by 1996. Capitalists competing for readers drove this expansion. (Jeffrey 2000: 98)

The second major transformation registered was in technology, with photocomposing and computerised typesetting replacing the hot metal process of the earlier era. This also swept way the bulky teleprinters that one senior reporter referred to as the nerve centre of news flow.

Among the tasks the Second Press Commission set for itself was that of examining in particular 'the present constitutional guarantee with regard to the freedom of the Press...' (*Report of the Second Press Commission* 1982, vol. 1: 2). Interestingly, it observed that 'regulation' must be distinguished from 'taking away' or 'abridgement' of the freedom of speech: 'Regulation does not hinder or curtail freedom of speech; in fact it can help promote freedom of speech. For freedom of speech to be meaningful in an assembly of persons, regulation of "speech" is absolutely essential if it were not to degenerate into a cacophony of words' (ibid.: 35). On the law of defamation, it made it a point to underline that the Constitution allows the imposition, by law, of reasonable restrictions on freedom of speech in relation to defamation (ibid.: 43).

What is conspicuous is the constant attempt by governments at the state and central level to enact laws designed to suppress media freedoms. In 1982, state governments in Bihar and Tamil Nadu passed laws that sought to punish journalists for publishing 'baseless' news; both pieces of legislation were either not passed by the president or repealed. In 1988, the Rajiv Gandhi government, already under pressure due to the Bofors scam and subjected to unrelenting press scrutiny over corruption charges, brought in the highly unpopular Defamation Bill.

The Second Press Commission's stance on defamation was cited by the government to justify the proposed legislation. But journalists' organisations were quick to call their bluff, as an eloquent statement put out by the Bombay Union of Journalists indicated:

> The Press Commission had taken the view that the truth of a statement should be sufficient defence against a charge of defamation and had rejected the suggestion that it should in addition be shown that the publication of the statement was in the public interest. Ignoring this important recommendation, the Defamation Bill requires that, in order to escape the charge of being defamatory, a statement must be both true and its publication must be shown to have been for the public good. (Bombay Union of Journalists 1988)

Not only did the Bill enlarge the definition of defamation, but also it introduced as a new category of offence 'the printing etc. of grossly indecent or scurrilous matter or matter intended for blackmail'. It is another matter that it was not a 'new category of offence' by any means. The ill-fated Press (Objectionable Matter) Act, 1951, repealed in 1957, had in fact brought under the category of 'objectionable matter' anything that was 'grossly indecent, or … scurrilous or obscene or intended for blackmail'!

The pushback against the Defamation Bill was unprecedented. It united mediapersons across the country—there were reportedly over a 100 public meetings organised by journalists. It also brought opposition parties, trade unions, teachers and ordinary citizens together in an unprecedented protest that saw for the first time in parliamentary history a law that had been passed in the Lok Sabha being junked. The *Economic and Political Weekly* editorialised: 'This climb down has without doubt been forced on him [Rajiv Gandhi] by the widespread and snowballing protests against his latest and extremely provocative attack on the democratic rights of the Indian people' (1988: 1868).

There have been other clashes too between governments and newspapers at the regional level. In the mid-1990s, for example, the Tamil Nadu government under Chief Minister J. Jayalalithaa clamped down on small publications critical of her functioning. So brutal was the assault that her police and party workers mounted on the printer of a local Tamil weekly, *Nakkeeran*, that he collapsed and died (Jeffrey 2000: 193). She also deployed the defamation law (Sections 499 and 500 of the IPC) on innumerable occasions against individual journalists and media houses (*Hindustan Times* 2016).

Economic Liberalisation and After

Veteran editors often expressed a sense of foreboding over the trajectory of print media, specifically the risk that it would become increasingly subservient to State power. But it was the exercise of corporate power that created the greatest consternation in the era of economic liberalisation. Wrote one editor, 'In pre-Independence days, the Press had a mission to rouse mass consciousness and serve the cause of freedom movement. Newspapers were run by national leaders of eminence who had indomitable courage and spirit of self-sacrifice.... Today, the Press is a business with a profit motive' (Sarkar 1984: 285).

Others traced the manner in which its economic restructuring during the early 1990s had rendered the media a 'muffled watchdog': 'Unlike in the pre-liberalization days, many media houses have established deeper intrinsic links with the corporate entities in different ways' (Raman 2018: 191). As Robin Jeffrey observes, 'Capitalism needs newspapers; newspapers spread to respond to capitalism; and in doing so, they help to make people into consumers and citizens' (2000: 210). He goes on to point out that while restrictions on foreign ownership protected Indian newspapers from global media proprietors, battles to capture readers, and therefore a larger share of the advertising pie, began to rage between big players within the country.

The Hindi heartland in the late 1980s and through the 1990s became a site of contending political ideologies fighting for supremacy. The assertion of the Other Backward Classes through Mandal politics, on the one hand, and the upper castes through Mandir politics, on the other, played out in the media space. The burgeoning circulation of Hindi newspapers bore testimony to this phenomenon: 'The nature of political developments in the heartland was not just mirrored in the media but in some sense was also mediated by it' (Ninan 2007: 217).

All this unfolded against the backdrop of economic restructuring. In the early 2000s, the Government of India allowed 26 per cent and 74 per cent foreign direct investment in the news and non-news print media respectively. By 2010, foreign direct investment in the media and entertainment sector had touched Rs 178.7 billion. The pressure of the market and capital flows had a direct impact on news reporting, blurring the traditional distinction between news and opinion and making more porous the boundaries between editorial and advertisement content (Philipose 2019: 37–38).

Also impacting independent reporting was a distinct rise in the use of defamation suits and court orders to target media freedom. The Constitution recognised, of course, that there must be reasonable restrictions on freedom of speech guarantees in relation to defamation. But over time media establishments became particularly vulnerable to such suits, often by powerful corporate interests. A series carried in *Rajasthan Patrika* in 2004 on the harmful impacts of pesticides drew the wrath of an umbrella body of pesticide manufacturers, Crop Care Federation, which claimed Rs 50 lakh in damages. Fortunately for the publication, the Delhi High Court recognised it as a SLAPP suit—an acronym for 'strategic lawsuits against public participation'—designed to intimidate the media from carrying articles of societal importance, and dismissed the case. But that reversal did not discourage the deployment of SLAPP suits against the media. In 2017, a Rs 100-crore case was brought against the respected journal, *Economic and Political Weekly* (*EPW*), by Adani Power Ltd for publishing a piece questioning whether it had evaded taxes to the tune of Rs 1,000 crore. The trustees of *EPW*, in this case, chose to take the piece down rather than fight the case in court.

Most democracies the world over have opted to banish criminal defamation from their statute books, even while many among them continued to recognise defamation as a civil crime. In India, despite many important court rulings against it, the law remains and, as recently as early 2024, the 22nd Law Commission recommended that criminal defamation be retained in India's criminal law. The chilling effect of these developments on journalism is very obvious. Investigative reporting has all but disappeared, or has been reduced to the recycling of documents supplied by vested interests.

There were other means also used to clamp down on the independent media. During the COVID-19 pandemic in

2020–2021, when the Government of India took a proactive stance in framing the public narrative, the Supreme Court passed an astonishing directive making it mandatory for news organisations to carry the government's version of any news related to the pandemic, citing the danger of fake news circulating at a critical time. The order caused a great deal of consternation among journalists, many of whom had had to face the government's wrath for reporting critically on the failures of the administration in addressing the unprecedented health crisis. The court order was seen to have 'been passed without a careful degree of appreciation of the contours of free expression, and what value it serves during the times of a pandemic' (Majumder 2023: 227).

Guardians of Independence Decline

Institutions set up in the 1950s and 1960s to safeguard newspaper independence themselves went into decline. Take the case of the Press Council of India, which was dissolved during the Emergency and reconstituted under the Press Council Act, 1978. One of the principal objectives of this law was to 'preserve the freedom of the Press and to maintain and improve the standards of newspapers and news agencies in India'. For a while, it was taken seriously by the newspaper establishment. One member who joined the Press Council in 1985 wrote:

> Cases involving some of the largest media houses were disposed of during our time. Often top Supreme Court lawyers had appeared before the inquiry committee to argue cases.... In B. G. Verghese v The Hindustan Times, the Council had passed a harsh judgement against the Birlas, the owners.... (Raman 2018: 182–183)

But that phase quickly ended: 'The harsh truth is that the Press Council, after the post-Emergency euphoria, has become an unwanted child. It main stake holders, ie media houses, did not feel comfortable with it' (Raman 2018: 183–184). This may be why a body that could have furthered media freedoms and pronounced on issues like exit polls, the Official Secrets Act and the floundering of small and medium newspapers, was allowed to go into decline. A telling instance of this was the manner in which attempts were made to suppress a major report on the phenomenon of paid news undertaken by Paranjoy Guha Thakurta, a member of the Press Council (Balaji 2010).

It fell to independent regulatory bodies instituted by journalists themselves to now display a greater appetite to analyse media-related developments and correct wrongs. The Editors' Guild of India, set up by veterans like Kuldip Nayar in 1978, has made several important interventions related to the coverage of pressing national issues. The Guild's fact-finding report of 2002 on the role of the media in fomenting the Gujarat pogrom, which continues to be an important source of information on that violence, is a case in point.[10] More recently, in 2023, it conducted a fact-finding mission on the mediatised aspects of the ethnic clashes that broke out in Manipur (Editors' Guild of India 2023).

But efforts such as these are few and far between and can do little about the structural infirmities of the print media. Observing the evolution of the Hindi media, Mrinal Pande notes that it began to give increased importance to political power, which in turn was utilised by many proprietors to expand their other businesses.

> Occasionally, guided by their political mentors, some publishers began to fine-tune the selection and promotion of embedded journalists. The earlier breed of editors at this point became somewhat redundant as editors began to be recruited on the basis of their proximity to the political party in power…. (Pande 2022: 81)

The fact was that a neoliberal order had little patience with principles that were seen as empty shibboleths. Media houses now preferred to set their own rules. The principle that journalism is 'a public service and a profession' now began to be regarded as anachronistic, and the editor was no longer the 'ear and eye' of a newspaper. 'The form and marketing of the "content" will be decided not by ethical press dharma prescribed by the Press Council but market surveys and consumer tastes and behaviour' (Raman 2018: 191–192).

The days of the First Press Commission, which wanted editors 'who can inspire all members of the team with their journalistic abilities as well as absolute integrity', have well and truly ended.

Notes

1. *Express Newspapers (Pvt) Ltd v. Union of India.* Available at https://indiankanoon.org/doc/891756/ (accessed February 2025).

2. *Express Newspapers* (1958).

3. *Sakal Papers (P) Ltd., And Others v. The Union Of India* 1961. Available at https://indiankanoon.org/doc/243002/ (accessed February 2025).

4. *Sakal Papers (P) Ltd., And Others v. The Union Of India* 1961.

5. *Bennett Coleman & Co v. Union of India & Ors*, 1972. Available at https://indiankanoon.org/doc/125596/ (accessed February 2025).

6. *Bennett Coleman & Co v. Union of India & Ors*, 1972.

7. *Bennett Coleman & Co v. Union of India & Ors*, 1972.

8. *Indian Express Newspapers v. Union Of India & Ors,* 1984. Available at https://indiankanoon.org/doc/223504/ (accessed February 2025).

9. *Ram Bahadur Rai v. The State Of Bihar & Ors*, 1974. Available at https://indiankanoon.org/doc/426727/ (accessed February 2025).

10. Excerpts of the report are publicly available. See https://cjp.org.in/editors-guild-fact-finding-mission-report-2002/ (accessed February 2025).

three

Radio, Television and Channelling Changing Ideas

Globally, radio and television have played a decisive role in amplifying free expression in both negative and positive ways. The 1994 genocide in Rwanda was triggered by two radio stations controlled by those in power: Radio Rwanda and Radio Télévision des Milles Collines (RTLM).[1] Six decades earlier, during the Spanish Civil War, it is said that Unión Radio Madrid kept people's morale going during the inhuman Francoist bombardments. Radios were played at full volume and the windows of houses were ordered to be kept open, in order to ensure that the greatest numbers could hear music and broadcasts (Acher 2022).

In India, the radio had its moments during the national movement. There was a time, for instance, when Usha Mehta along with Babubhai Vithalbhai and their colleagues ran clandestine broadcasts from a Bombay apartment during the Quit India movement, calling themselves the 'Voice of Freedom, speaking from somewhere in India'. These were in Hindi and English, recorded in Bombay and begun as two daily broadcasts. Later this was brought down to once a day, in the late evening. Mehta would recall that news came to them from across the country through special messengers and they could often put out information crucial for the freedom movement that the newspapers did not, or could not, carry; information such as, for instance, how rice merchants, heeding the national call, were refusing to export their grain. Messages from Gandhi and other leaders, along with reports on their speeches, were also put out. The authorities cracked down on this brave effort within four months, yet during the short span of time that the Voice of Freedom could function, it did demonstrate the immense potential of the radio to rally participation in the nationalist movement and uphold people's right to freedom of expression (*BBC* 2020).

The post-independence Indian State, which had inherited six AIR stations from the erstwhile British Raj, also inherited the instinct to wield the medium for State purposes. The assumption that radio would be controlled by the State was never challenged, and the medium came to be viewed as a tool to forge a nationalism envisaged as cooperative federalism held together by a strong centre. All broadcasting, in fact, both radio and later television, came under two colonial laws, the Indian Telegraph Act of 1885 and the Indian Wireless Telegraphy Act of 1933, which made it clear that the Government of India had sole jurisdiction and oversight over all forms of communications, both wired and wireless, within the territory of India.

In 1956, AIR was renamed Akashvani (literally, 'voice from the sky'), in a bid to rid it of its colonial legacy. What remained intact, of course, was its utter subservience to government diktat. The post-independence State was very committed to a controlled and guided radio and the nomenclature given to the ministry which was to oversee and regulate the entire media in India featured the word 'Broadcasting' prominently. The Ministry of Information and Broadcasting (MIB) was instituted on the very first day of Independence. It must be noted that at that point of time, radio broadcasting covered only 2.5 per cent of the Indian landmass and 11 per cent of the population, with the total number of radio sets at 2,75,000 (Prasar Bharati n. d.).

Total Government Control

Government control over broadcasting media seriously compromised the Indian citizen's constitutional right to freedom of speech and expression. This is particularly so because radio, and later television, given their capacity to capture mass attention, are important modes of exercising power.

The political justification made in newly independent India for total governmental monopoly over the medium was that it would help unite a multi-ethnic, multi-religious country ravaged by a grim Partition, and contribute to its 'development'. Additionally, there was a patina of patriotism that hung over the radio—it was argued that unlike the press of the era it was not in search of profits and existed solely to disseminate information on government policies, programmes and projects. For the radio, according to those who administered it, 'The most important task was to ensure that the output of programs was clear, entertaining, educational, informative, and intelligible, with the aim of fostering a national mindset and culture' (Kripalani 2017: 40).

There were other moments when the radio did play a crucial role in the country's evolution as a republic. During the first general election conducted in 1951–52, AIR was put to good use in building awareness on the importance of casting one's vote and how one may do so. The voter turnout was modest—45.7 per cent—compared to contemporary levels, but considering that this was the first such exercise in a newly independent nation, it was a commendable performance and it was widely recognised that the proliferation of information at a pan-India level through the air waves was central to this outcome. As one commentator put it, 'The success of these efforts was evident by the huge voter turnout and the conduct of a free and fair election' (Kripalani 2017: 40).

The majority of radio coverage in the country was through single-channel, medium-wave stations. Therefore the programmes had to be of a composite nature, catering to the tastes of a variety of audience groups.

> In the post-Independence decades, radios blared from every street corner shop, home, and, with the coming of the transistor radio in the 1960s, every passing bicycle.... Music programs were interspersed with news broadcasts, commentaries, and interviews. As there was primarily only one station, everyone mostly listened to the same program. (Kripalani 2017: 40)

Besides, the stations also had to conform to policy directives and instructions from the central broadcasting organisation and the MIB. All this allowed very little scope for creativity in programming. Many of the programmes were about 'nation-building' and farming was a significant theme: 'Farmers received timely weather advisories and could even take courses on agriculture via radio. All this was important in helping India achieve the famous 1960s agricultural Green Revolution that ended famine in India' (ibid.: 42).

Such an arrangement, one that made the radio a mouthpiece of the government, challenged the constitutional notion of freedom of expression. Long after it became increasingly apparent that the radio was being used by the central government for its own propaganda, in direct violation of the citizen's constitutional right of freedom of information, it was still projected as an effort to ensure that citizens of the country received unbiased news.

Limited though the scale of radio was in the early years of independence, the government took it seriously. In fact, the radio was the sole form of mass media that existed at that point, given that newspapers had modest circulations and reached a relatively low number of Indians, most of whom happened to be city dwellers. On 3 December 1949, a few weeks before the nation's first Republic Day, Prime Minister Jawaharlal Nehru told the people of India that he wanted to keep in touch with them, 'if not in person at least through the radio' (*The Times of India* 1949). Although Nehru was not particularly good at keeping this promise, moments of national import did occasion a radio address. A particularly poignant instance of this was Nehru coming on air to tell the people of India about the Indo-China war of 1962:

> Comrades, friends and fellow countrymen. I am speaking to you on the radio after a long interval. I feel however that I must speak to you about the grave situation that has arisen on our frontiers because of continuing and unabashed aggression by Chinese forces…. (McDemott et al. 2015: 737)

While his form of address to his radio audience was far from intimate, almost Western in tone, there was some truth to W. H. Morris-Jones' observation that Nehru 'rules a country of continental size and bewildering diversities with a microphone' (Sen 2021).

The prime ministers who followed him also realised the enormous value of the medium and used it to convey their thoughts and ideas to a pan-national audience at crucial junctures of the country's history. After the anti-Hindi riots that broke out in Tamil Nadu in 1965, Lal Bahadur Shastri, through a speech broadcast by AIR on 11 February 1965, conveyed the pledge that Hindi would not be imposed and that the use of English by the government would not be discontinued. He made it a point to speak in English in deference to Tamil sentiments on that occasion (Guha 2020).

Policy-making in those early days bore vestiges of the bitterness of Partition. This was most marked when it came to deciding the language that was to be used for the broadcasts in northern India. The earlier compromise of an admixture of Urdu and Hindi, in what came to known as Hindustani, was steadily undermined with the growing use of a highly Sanskritised Hindi. It is important to flag this choice of language while considering issues of freedom of expression. The point is that the arbitrary imposition of a particular lexicon had enormous implications for the right of listeners to receive information and express cultural patterns of secular life. The content of even music broadcasts on AIR was studiously controlled. As a media scholar noted, 'Ministers of Information and Broadcasting, Sardar Vallabhbhai Patel until 1950 and then B.V. Keskar (1952–1962), sought to zealously protect All India Radio from the "tawaifi" Muslim music. This, coming against the backdrop of a concerted move to cleanse AIR of Muslim and Urdu influence, led to the resignation of its first Director General, Ahmed Shah Bukhari' (Kumar 2013).

When television was introduced to Indian audiences on an experimental basis in September 1959, it was a service offered by AIR. Named Doordarshan, the service had an extremely modest and uncertain start, comprising an unprepossessing studio, a low-powered transmitter and some two dozen community television sets. Since the mood within the government was that of abstemiousness, the general perception in policy circles at the time was that television was too much of a luxury for a poor country like India and not much investment was to be wasted on it. This of course was to change as we will see later in this chapter.

First Independent Review of Radio Functioning

Both radio and television were ringfenced by the MIB and this had obvious and severely negative implications for the citizen's constitutional right to freedom of expression. This state of affairs riled up the opposition parties greatly and it was their loud and persistent criticism of the lack of independence of the national broadcaster that ultimately led to an important step being taken by the government in 1964: the setting up of the A. K. Chanda Committee. It was the first independent review of its kind and its primary responsibility was to inquire into the functioning of Akashvani and Doordarshan.

The Chanda Committee Report was formally presented to the government two years later in 1966. The report did engage in some plain speaking about the state of affairs, noting that ministerial interference was constant and influenced not just policy-making and programming but even staff selection. It also observed that AIR was timid in reporting, put out stale news (1966: 96–97), required a 'psychological transformation' and was underfunded (Shrivastava 1989: 21). It also recommended that radio and television operations be bifurcated.

While the Chanda Committee Report was not implemented, it did to an extent influence subsequent policy. The suggestion that Akashvani and Doordarshan become separate entities was put in place a decade later when the two entities were given their own distinct offices, budget outlays and staff. The report had argued that radio must become more accessible to those living in rural areas and this was in sync with ongoing governmental efforts. The Third Five Year Plan (1961–66) had mandated the expansion of AIR's medium-wave internal services coverage, from 37 per cent of the total area of the country and 55 per cent of its population to 61 per cent of area and 74 per cent of the population (Government of India 1961: 571).

The AIR Code, which was finalised with the Cabinet's approval in 1967 and amended in March 1970, also drew tangentially from suggestions made in the Chanda Committee Report. The Code laid down norms for content, proscribing inter alia criticism of friendly countries, attacks on religions or communities and material that was obscene, defamatory or which incited violence or amounted to contempt of court. Care was also taken to include strictures against the misuse of electronic media to favour a particular party; while attacks on a political party by name were prohibited, so too was hostile criticism of the state and central governments.

Among the reasons why the Chanda Committee's report got short shrift was a significant shift in the political scenario in the two years since its inception. It was set up when Indira Gandhi happened to be the Union minister of information and broadcasting but by the time the report came out she had become the country's prime minister and was rather less inclined to liberalise the operations of State media. In fact, her impulse was the opposite of this, if we are to go by her record of media censorship during the Emergency she imposed on the country in 1975 (an aspect already noted in Chapter 2). There were other factors too that militated against substantial reform at this juncture. The timing of the report was inopportune, as Robin Jeffrey was to observe: 'Prime Minister, Lal Bahadur Shastri, had died in January, Mrs Gandhi was an unsteady replacement, the country had just fought its second war in three years and the two-year "Bihar famine" was beginning' (cited in *MediaClassification.org*).

Emergency and its Impact on Broadcasting

During the Emergency the joke was that so faithfully did the national broadcaster project the prime minister that AIR was termed 'All Indira Radio' while Doordarshan was given the moniker of 'Devidarshan'. Indira Gandhi was believed to be extremely fastidious about how she came across on radio and television. One of her advisors would later recall that the longest and most tedious meetings with her inevitably involved the preparation of her speeches. One of them, broadcast on the midnight of 3 December 1971 after India declared war on Pakistan, had to be revised several times at the last moment until she was fully satisfied (Sen 2021).

The 21 months of the Emergency saw government control over the national broadcaster tighten in an unprecedented manner. A white paper on 'Misuse of the Mass Media', prepared by the Government of India, which came out in August 1977—after the defeat of Indira Gandhi in a general election—documented the full extent of this misuse. Within six months of the declaration of the Emergency on 25 June 1975, there were 'no less than 197 instructions issued by the Directorate General, All India Radio, to Station Directors' with regard to 'content, periodicity and presentation of programmes dealing with the 20-Point Programme' (Government of India 1977: 66). It noted that a sustained effort was made to project the prime minister in a positive light to national audiences. Most of her speeches were repeatedly broadcast and 301 quotations from them were repeated in broadcasts from all stations during gaps between programmes. It was not just Mrs Gandhi but also her son, Sanjay Gandhi, who was accorded such extraordinary attention. Between 1 January 1976 and 18 January 1977, there were no fewer than 192 bulletins carried in the main news section, most of them repetitive, inane and devoid of news content, such as continuous references made to 'Shri Gandhi' being welcomed by excited crowds in various cities (Kapoor 2015: 66).

Live coverage of developments on the ground was also severely compromised. The violent incidents at Turkman Gate, Delhi, to take one instance, were ignored in news bulletins and a doctored version of what had transpired was carried later. Bureaucrats often made a difficult atmosphere worse due to their anxiety to be seen to be doing the right thing. Ameen Sayani, who was closely associated with the radio for decades, tells the story of the song 'Mehengai Maar Gai' ('the soaring prices are killing us') from the film *Roti Kapda Aur Makaan*, which was banned by AIR during this period 'because someone high up in Delhi wasn't comfortable with people being informed that "prices were hitting the roof"!' (Sayani 2020).

What was perhaps the most salient recommendation of the Chanda Committee—the granting of autonomy to Akashvani and Doordarshan—expectedly found no favour with the Indira Gandhi government. It was only after her defeat in 1977 that the B. G. Verghese Committee was set up under the Janata government. Verghese in his memoir characterises that assignment as one of the most stimulating that had ever come his way: 'After many hearings and visits we had recommended [the] establishment of a National Broadcast Trust named Akash Bharati, responsible for the conduct of public broadcasting' (2010: 259–260). It was to be equipped with a charter, a board and a full-time controller general of broadcasting.

In its report, which came out in February 1978, the Verghese Committee referenced the experience of media capture during the Emergency, observing: 'the executive, abetted by a captive parliament, shamelessly misused broadcasting during [the] emergency and this must be prevented for all times' (*The Hindu* 2018). It was for this reason, it argued, that an independent corporation with constitutional safeguards was essential for ensuring independent broadcasting services. But equipping the proposed body with constitutional safeguards, over which the legislature had no control, was a step too far for even the Janata Party. Verghese later recalled that L. K. Advani, the Union minister for information and broadcasting at that time, 'wryly exclaimed, "We promised autonomy. But you have recommended independence"' (Verghese 2010: 260).

That courageous effort was unsurprisingly put on ice. The excruciatingly slow progress of the idea of autonomous broadcasting through the political labyrinth over the next four and a half decades is comment enough on the extraordinary difficulties in translating the seemingly simple formulation 'freedom of speech and expression' into reality.

Autonomous National Broadcaster?

When Advani introduced the Prasar Bharati Bill in May 1979, which envisaged an institution with 'genuine autonomy' to govern AIR and Doordarshan, he made sure that the proposal for constitutional safeguards suggested by the Verghese Committee did not figure in its architecture. It did, though, expand the definition of broadcasting to mean 'the dissemination of any form of communication like signs, signals, writing, pictures, images and sounds of all kinds by transmission of electromagnetic waves through space as through cables indeed to be received by the general public, either directly or indirectly through the medium of relay stations and all its grammatical variations and cognate expressions shall be construed accordingly' (Section 2c).[2]

A report that appeared in a contemporary newspaper revealed that 'a government spokesperson admitted that the chairman of Prasar Bharati (Broadcasting Corporation of India) will have no option but to follow the central directives. However, he felt such directives will be 'few and far between' (*Indian Express* 2019 [1979]). It went on to say:

> According to an analysis of the Bill circulated among newsmen, the government's power to give directives could not be restricted to

> national security and other matters of grave public importance since it would be necessary 'to correct any aberrations' from the charter of objectives of the corporation. (*Indian Express* 2019 [1979])

Seven months later, Indira Gandhi won the general election in 1981 and returned to power. With the change of government the Prasar Bharati Bill of 1979 also lapsed and the new Congress government studiedly made no effort to reintroduce it. However, the dissatisfaction over the government's tight control of the national broadcaster did not by any means disappear. Even the P. C. Joshi Committee, set up by the Indira Gandhi government to provide a software template for Doordarshan in 1983, noted that the lack of 'functional freedom' was having an adverse effect on the planning and quality of its programmes. Its report, which came out in 1985 when Rajiv Gandhi was the prime minister, noted that although the government had not accepted the Verghese Committee's recommendations of statutory autonomy for Akashvani and Doordarshan, its spokespersons had said they were for functional freedom for the two organisations, and it urged the government to ensure this.[3]

Despite these well-argued representations, every attempt to ensure greater autonomy in the years that followed came against the iron will of the government to control broadcasting. The National Front government, under V. P. Singh, once again revived the idea of the Prasar Bharati Bill in December 1989, and the Prasar Bharati (Broadcasting Corporation of India) Act was enacted by Parliament in 1990 after innumerable amendments. One of the major concerns was whether both AIR and Doordarshan should come under a common structure. Verghese recalled, 'After much deliberation, it was felt that it would be best to keep both under a single agency in view of commonalities and shared overheads. A unified body would also ensure that radio was not neglected, an assumption sadly belied' (Verghese 2010: 364).

Section 12 of the Act laid out the functions and powers of the Corporation, stating that the 'primary duty of the Corporation [was] to organise and conduct public broadcasting services to inform, educate and entertain the public and to ensure a balanced development of broadcasting on radio and television'. This section took care to underline that the Corporation would continue to be ruled by the provisions of the Indian Telegraph Act, 1885.

A long list of objectives was also outlined, ranging from 'upholding the unity and integrity of the country and the values enshrined in the Constitution' and 'presenting a fair and balanced flow of information including contrasting views without advocating any opinion or ideology of its own' to 'providing adequate coverage to the diverse cultures and languages of the various regions of the country by broadcasting appropriate programmes'; 'informing and stimulating the national consciousness in regard to the status and problems of women and paying special attention to the upliftment of women'; 'promoting social justice and combating exploitation, inequality and such evils as untouchability and advancing the welfare of the weaker sections of the society' and 'promoting national integration by broadcasting in a manner that facilitates communication in the languages in India; and facilitating the distribution of regional broadcasting services in every State in the languages of that State'. Figuring high on this list was the Corporation's mandate to 'safeguard the citizen's right to be informed freely, truthfully and objectively on all matters of public interest'.

The Act was to come into force on 1 April 1991, but by then the Congress had withdrawn support to the Chandra Shekhar government and it had lost its authority to rule. It formally collapsed that June, as did the new law.

Prasar Bharati had become something of an albatross for political parties across the board. While they wanted to project themselves as votaries of freedom of speech and expression, allowing the national broadcaster total freedom remained too lofty a goal for their purposes. Two cases from this period indicate just how lofty that goal really was. Doordarshan refused to broadcast Anand Patwardhan's award-winning 1990 film on violence in Punjab, *In Memory of Friends*, which led him to go to court. In 1992, the Bombay High Court ruled that the filmmaker had the right to put his views before the people and the public had the right to be so informed. That year also saw the Supreme Court criticise Doordarshan for its refusal to air *Bhopal Beyond Genocide*, an award-winning documentary by Tapan Bose, ruling that the national broadcaster could not refuse to show this film without seriously infringing on the right to free speech.

The More Things Change …

Under the Congress government of Narasimha Rao (1991–1996), we had the Union minister of information and broadcasting, K. P. Singh Deo, frankly express his quandary over autonomy to Doordarshan. When asked by a reporter what was to be the modified form of Prasar Bharati that his government was considering, he replied, 'Earlier, there was a provision that the Government can direct Prasar Bharati to broadcast something in the national interest. Now that has been expanded—we've proposed that the Government can stop a programme from being telecast too' (*India Today* 1994). The more things threatened to change, the more they remained the same. The government did, however, set up a committee in time-honoured fashion under Nitesh Sengupta in December 1995, which suggested that Akashvani and Doordarshan be completely independent of each other although both would come under the Prasar Bharati Corporation.

The non-Congress government that followed ensured that Prasar Bharati became a statutory autonomous body in November 1997, through an ordinance passed under the United Front government of I. K. Gujral, for whom it must have been a moment of epiphany, a chance to discard the authoritarian reputation that had clung to him from his days as information and broadcasting minister in the early period of the Emergency. But even non-Congress governments, although they seemed eager to resurrect Prasar Bharati time and again, would fail the test of ensuring true autonomy for the institution when things came to a crunch.

Days after the Gujral government breathed life into Prasar Bharati, his government collapsed. The new National Democratic Alliance (NDA) government under Prime Minister Atal Bihari Vajpayee allowed the Prasar Bharati Ordinance passed by the Gujral government to lapse and promptly brought its own ordinance with a singular intent to get rid of its independent-minded chief executive officer, S. S. Gill, appointed by the earlier government. This was done by fixing an age limit for the post and thereby disqualifying him. An opposition party spokesman described the move as unconstitutional in procedure, undemocratic in terms of ideology and unethical in terms of values (*Tribune* 1998), yet it reflected the near impossibility of ensuring that Prasar Bharati remained independent of executive control. Verghese's dream of an autonomous Prasar Bharati, accountable only to Parliament, was a non-starter. 'Autonomy was never given; it needed to be grasped. This the board failed to do', he commented (Verghese 2010: 481).

In 2000, the Vajpayee government appointed the Shunu Sen Committee, which had several recommendations to make, especially on hiring practices and funding mechanisms. In a reply in Parliament to a question on whether the government accepted the recommendations of the committee, then minister of information and broadcasting, Arun Jaitley, was evasive: 'View on some of the recommendations of the Committee is to be taken by Prasar Bharati, whereas in respect of some others, Government has to take a view.'[4]

The pattern was set. Every time officers asserted themselves and tried to run the organisation according to its mandate, they were turfed out. The Prasar Bharati Board had, for instance, appointed S. Y. Quraishi, a bureaucrat of some credibility, as a full-time director-general of Doordarshan in 2001. Within two years he was quietly removed, with no reasons for the decision being cited. The two terms under the United Progressive Alliance (UPA), from 2004 to 2014, did not witness any major change in the pattern of executive capture. Early in its second term, the Manmohan Singh government prepared a report on the dysfunctionality of Prasar Bharati as an institution, noting particularly the turf wars that had broken out between the Board and the CEO. The question of whether the government was considering passing another ordinance to dismiss the board was very much in the air, but the government remained cryptic on the matter. 'It would be very difficult to comment now on what step we will take regarding this issue,' a source informed *The Indian Express* (2009).

The UPA government in early 2013 constituted yet another committee under Sam Pitroda to suggest, inter alia, 'measures to sustain, strengthen and amplify Prasar Bharati's role as a Public Broadcaster'. The Report of the expert committee came out just before the general election of 2014. Its recommendations were ambitious, beginning with the suggestion that it should become a 'genuine public broadcaster', not a 'government broadcaster' and to achieve this recommended that the Prasar Bharati Act, 1990, be amended to make for 'effective freedom' so that it could frame rules and regulations, as well as hire personnel without government approval (*Report of the Expert Committee on Prasar Bharati* 2014). This sudden desire by the Manmohan Singh government for a truly anonymous Prasar Bharati was almost certainly driven by an anxiety over imminent defeat.

The NDA-II Era

As things turned out, NDA, the opposition alliance came to power in 2014 under Narendra Modi. The recommendations of the Pitroda Committee were placed on the backburner but it was only a matter of time before the institution once again became the focus of the new government's attention. Since the 13-member Prasar Bharati board is the lynchpin in the Prasar Bharati architecture, with the directors of both Akashvani and Doordarshan having to report to it, the modus operandi adopted was familiar. In October 2015, four BJP appointees were inducted into the board, with the young minister of information and broadcasting, Rajyavardhan Rathore, not even bothering to wait for the nomination committee to announce the names before making the list of inductees public (*The Wire* 2015).

The government, in the last year of its first term, toyed seriously with 'exploring possible models to run the two bodies under it, Doordarshan (DD) and All India Radio (AIR), including converting them into public sector companies' (*The Print* 2018). Prasar Bharati is totally dependent on the MIB for its funding, and the fear of the government pulling the plug was real. In March 2018, the chairperson of Prasar Bharati did go public with the fact that the MIB had been withholding funds and the organisation had had to draw from its contingency funds to pay salaries to its employees. This was a problem that kept recurring from time to time, indicating the instability of the entire financial model of the institution. In addition, the government then came up with a draft of a Prasar Bharati Amendment Bill, under which the MIB was to be given the power to appoint directors to Akashvani and Doordarshan, which would actually amount to shelving the idea of an autonomous national broadcaster.

After it came back to power for a second term in 2019, there was little evidence of any real autonomy in the functioning of Prasar Bharati. News bulletins faithfully followed the government line, just as they had done in the mid-1970s. There was the additional aspect of Prasar Bharati having drawn even closer to the ruling party apparatus. Three developments pointed to this. *First*, the prime minister was allowed a monthly personal broadcast, 'Mann ki Baat', starting October 2014, which clearly created conditions of bias in favour of the executive.[5] *Second*, among its board members were those closely associated with the ruling party: Ashok Kumar Tandon, former head of the prime minister's office (PMO) under Atal Bihari Vajpayee, and Shaina N. C., a BJP spokesperson. *Third*, some of its policy decisions followed the ruling party's ideological orientation. In 2023, for instance, it was decided that Prasar Bharati would stop relying on feeds from a professional news agency like the Press Trust of India, and instead depend on Hindustan Samachar, which had close links to the RSS (*Scroll.in* 2023). In April 2024, the logo of Doordarshan News assumed a saffron hue. But it was not just the logo. A recent scrutiny of 42 segments of the 9 PM news show, *Do Took*, revealed that the majority of these segments (59.5 per cent) targeted the Opposition, 'misinformation and disinformation' marked a significant number of them (28 per cent) and communal polarisation was very evident in at least 7.1 per cent of them (Singh 2024). Thus the 20-point programme of Prasar Bharati, advocating balanced news presentation and the prohibition of communally polarising content, seemed to have become totally hollowed out.

While it is uncontestable that the constitutional guarantee of freedom of expression requires autonomy for the national broadcaster, the vexed history of the Prasar Bharati experiment indicates the impossibly high threshold of difficulty in achieving such an objective. One of the sections of the Prasar Bharati Act, 1990, made it clear that a central objective of the Act was to safeguard 'the citizen's right to be informed freely, truthfully and objectively on all matters of public interest, national or international, and presenting a fair and balanced flow of information including contrasting views without advocating any opinion or ideology of its own'. Unfortunately, going by the experience on the ground, it appears to be as difficult to achieve autonomy for the national broadcaster as it is to ensure freedom of expression for citizens!

The other dimension was commercialisation. The Chanda Committee in its 1966 Report had recommended that Akashvani be opened up to commercial interests in order to be able to sustain itself financially at least partially, although there were concerns that commercial stakeholders, with their interest in creating mass audiences for advertisers, could dilute Akashvani's original vision of 'informing and educating the masses'. Entertaining them was also part of the deal but that had always been placed lower in the list of priorities. Nevertheless, Vividh Bharati, dedicated to film music, made its appearance on a permanent basis in 1977, after being broadcast on a trial basis for a year. Two decades later a few frequencies in the FM radio range were made available to private players but it was not until 1993, after Narasimha Rao move to liberalise and globalise the economy, that FM radio frequencies were auctioned to private producers.

Those who benefitted from the move hailed it enthusiastically. Commercial broadcaster, the late Ameen Sayani, was to recall: 'Listeners still remember the sudden breath of fresh air brought in by the informal, fun-filled, chatty programmers of Radio Mid-Day and Times FM from the morning of 15 August 1993' (Sayani 2020). FM Radio was also allowed to seek foreign funds that constitute not more that 49 per cent of its total budgetary provision. Revised policy guidelines, announced in 2005, specified that broadcasters were to be allowed a free hand when it came to the quantum of advertising. Interestingly, the following year saw policy guidelines being issued for community radio services, which specified that advertisements and public announcements could not account for more than five minutes in an hour of broadcasting, and the excess funds so gained would have to be used to meet running costs. The contrast between the two models could not have been starker. One commentator observed that when it came to the allocation of frequencies for FM radio broadcasting, the government seemed to view the airwaves as a public resource to be auctioned off to the highest corporate bidder. The vast majority of licenses were granted to well-established media companies. 'Entertainment Networks (India), a company owned by the Times of India group, won 25 FM radio broadcast circles, to add to the seven that it was running under its brand name, Radio Mirchi' (Muralidharan 2007: 747).

No Independent News on Private Radio

What successive governments did veto, however, was the independent broadcasting of news and current affairs, whether on commercial radio or community radio, making India one of the few democratic countries in the world in which the government continues to control news. Not opening up FM radio to news not only violated Article 19(1)(a), it went against court verdicts which ruled that freedom of speech and expression included within its ambit not only volume of circulation but also volume of news and views (*Report of the Radio Broadcast Policy Committee* 2003). Those FM radio stations that sought a news component to their programming were allowed only to draw on the news bulletins of Akashvani.

The government offered many explanations for keeping independent radio news out of bounds for privately controlled radio. That it could potentially compromise India's 'security' was one of them. It was even argued that the FM mode was best utilised for music. But arguably the most outrageous reason proffered was that since the radio reaches vulnerable minds at the grassroots, it could mean that masses will be swayed by any information, including false information. As one critic put it, this line of reasoning assumed that most Indians did not have the capacity to make their own choices: 'To deny them, on an easily accessible medium such as the radio, a broad spectrum of information to enable them to make considered choices is to take away from the sanctity and right of that exercise of franchise' (Kumar 2013).

Former director general of AIR, P. C. Chatterji was of the same view: 'To have access to all shades of opinion through the medium of broadcasting is the right of every individual in India, and is provided for under the very article of the Constitution which guarantees freedom of thought and expression and ensures a free press' (1987: 183). He stated unequivocally that the government, by insisting on maintaining a monopoly of news, was violating a fundamental right guaranteed under the Constitution.

Television Outpaces Radio

When television was introduced to Indian audiences on an experimental basis in September 1959, it came under All India Radio services as we saw earlier in this chapter. There was no television manufacturing industry in the country at that point and importing the technology was prohibitive, especially after the 1962 India–China War which had led to an extreme shortage of foreign exchange.

By the mid-1960s, television programming had grown but was still very basic, nothing much beyond something for farmers ('Krishi Darshan'), and something by way of 'entertainment' ('Chitrahaar' and a weekly film). The 1965 war with Pakistan highlighted for leaders in India the need to buttress the country's television presence for propaganda reasons. This led to television stations being set up in the border cities of Srinagar and Amritsar.

Despite the hesitation to invest more comprehensively in television media, many technocrats of the era recognised it as the sleeping giant it was. Vikram Sarabhai, who helped set up for the country's first geostationary satellite system to serve India's telecommunication and television requirements, noted that

> television can be a most important tool for development. In this context, its impact is at least as relevant, if not more so, to the isolated rural communities where the bulk of our population resides as it is to the urban population already subject to other major influences of modernization … audio-visual experiences, can be a most important factor for national integration. (Sarabhai 1970)

It was the transfer of satellite technology from the US to India in 1975, possibly driven by a combination of US's own geo-strategic interests and its search for global markets, that eventually transformed the medium at home. The driving force, however, was the ambition of the Indian Space Research Organisation (ISRO) and technocrats like Sarabhai to develop satellite communication in India.

Sarabhai promoted a National Satellite Communication Group in 1968, and based on its recommendation, the Indian government finally adopted the idea of a hybrid television network comprising communication satellites as well as ground-based relay transmitters—[the] aim being to disseminate messages across a wide audience at the lowest possible cost (Shah 2019: 8).

Whatever the motivations, the US loaned for a year its ATS-6 satellite which ensured that the Satellite Instructional Television Experiment (SITE) project could reach Indian audiences. By 1976, 2,400 villages in six states were receiving educational television programmes. That year, at the height of the Emergency, the Republic Day Parade and Beating of the Retreat were telecast live. The next stage came when a Franco-German satellite, Syphonie-1, was deployed in 1977–1979 to lay the parameters of a possible domestic satellite system. This was followed by a series of multipurpose geostationary satellites launched by ISRO known as INSAT I and INSAT II.

Commercial TV

The commercial dimension of television broadcasting was the elephant in the room. For the moment it appeared that the constitutional imperative of national integration and the guarantee of right to free expression trumped the market imperative:

> The idea of an INSAT system had been first proposed in the late 1960s. The common plan on which various concepts of the system rested was the 'potential of the satellite medium can be drawn upon

for rapid expansion of TV on a nationwide basis for education, national integration and development'. (Sengupta 1996)

In fact, at that point there was no market to speak of, in any case. State television plodded on with an agenda of development, some of which ended up glorifying the coercive sterilisation drives seen during the Emergency but failed considerably in capturing viewer interest at a mass level. The documentary-style realism of its well-meaning but dreary programmes went well with the notion of 'the state television's investment in the Nehruvian social agendas of development and "national integration"' (Sen and Roy 2014: 27).

Doordarshan's first commercial programme in dull black and white was a bit like a pebble dropping in a large pond—it created very few ripples. What did change the outlook somewhat was the onset of colour. INSAT 1A came at a time when the government was searching for ways to amplify the Asiad Games it was hosting in Delhi in 1982: 'Watching the Games on a colour set was considered a privilege almost equal to watching the event live' (Shah 2019: 36). Suddenly, while every middle class family wanted a colour set, the reality was that 80 per cent of television sets manufactured in India were B&W ones. It was around this time that there was a sharp rightward shift in economic policy. This was reflected in the actions of successive governments, whether it was the $500 million IMF loan that Mrs Gandhi sought, or the decision of her son, Rajiv Gandhi, to expand industrial capacities and strike collaborations with transnational corporations.

Initially, both within the government and Doordarshan, there was a strong resistance to commercialisation and to sponsored programmes. The belief was that as long as sponsoring of programmes were not allowed, Indian television would not go the way of its Western counterparts (Mirchandani 1976: 35). But the ideological lines came to be sharply drawn—the state-controlled broadcaster, mandated to 'usher in development' through its programmes, was now pitted against a model driven by aggressive consumerism and in search of ever larger audiences to attract advertisers. While print media, as we saw, had long confronted this reality, it was now the turn of the visual media to do so. Before long, advertising came to drive the growth and evolution of commercial television in the country.

It was at this juncture that '[f]or 78 weeks, between 1987 and 1988, India, courtesy Doordarshan, was hooked on a heavenly opiate' (Shah 2019: 87), Ramanand Sagar's *Ramayana*, which brought it not just saturation viewership but unprecedented riches from advertising—its first run alone brought in an estimated Rs 23 crore. But the serial had consequences that went far beyond just revenue. Media academic Arvind Rajagopal, tracing the intertwining of culture and politics in his much-cited analysis, *Politics after Television* (2001), noted that it provided a fillip to popular Hindutva and helped trigger the rise of the BJP. The ideological underpinnings of the serial did raise questions about whether the national broadcaster should be promoting what was without doubt a serial soaked in majoritarian religiosity.

This question was to be revisited over a decade later when popular television serials like *Kyunki Saas Bhi Kabhi Bahu Thi* popularised a specific image of women as opulently dressed domestic goddesses with a very distinct Hindu identity. While their brocaded saris and the glowing sindoor on their foreheads may appear to be an attempt to reach out to tradition, they were in fact, as gender academic Purnima Mankekar points out, 'representations of aspects of modernity, in particular capitalistic modernity, as something to aspire to for the future' (Mankekar 2014: 52).

Liberalisation and Television

In 1991, the Narasimha Rao government ushered in economic liberalisation, intensifying the flows into India of global capital, culture, commodities, information and technologies. The constitutional right of free expression took on new shades of meaning, based on the logic of the market. The figures told the story: In 1971, 16 B&W television sets were being manufactured, but by 1988 India was producing 1,300 colour television sets in addition to 4,400 B&W ones (Bhartur 1989). By 1992, the number of people clustering around a television set would have been a little over 26. By 2006, the ratio had come down to 10. In a little over a decade, the total number of Indian TV households tripled to reach 112 million (Mehta 2014: 149). This in turn transformed both the medium and the message, both content creation and consumer tastes and ultimately a demographic emerged that came to be termed the 'new middle class' (Fernandes 2006).

There were innovative attempts made by private capital to get around government control of television. In the early 1990s the magazine group, *India Today*, set up a video news magazine, *Newstrack*, that would exploit the booming video market in the country, although it had to contend with State censorship (Singh 1992: xiv).

Newstrack pointed to a wholly new challenge that Doordarshan had to face: changing technologies. Television gave rise to a video boom, with the court recognising in 1989 that cable television constituted 'public viewing'. An estimated 1,000 cable operators in Bombay were using pirated videos by 1989 (Shah 2019: 60). The government responded by passing the Cable Television Network (Regulation) Act in 1995, which set down norms for uplinking and downlinking, and included a Programme Code and Advertising Code. It recognised cable operators as legal entities, provided they conformed to these codes. Yet enforcing these codes was an impossible task because they are defined very broadly and vaguely. On the one hand, they allowed much room for State censorship; on the other, given the enormous clout wielded by big players in a chaotic market, normative frameworks were quickly discarded. Suggestions that television needs to follow the agenda points from the Beijing Platform for Action (1995) by providing 'gender-sensitive training for media professionals' and 'encouraging the creation and use of non-stereotyped, balanced and diverse images of women in the media' or promoting the idea that 'sexist stereotypes displayed in the media are gender discriminatory, degrading in nature and offensive' never got translated into policy.

TV News Goes Commercial

Amidst this chaos, the Government of India tried hard to hold on to its hegemony over news broadcasting, as it had done with radio, but failed conspicuously. Television academic Nalin Mehta tells the story of how Prime Minister Narasimha Rao vetoed a live current affairs programme on DD3 because it was 'too dangerous'. He pointed out that control over television was central to and constitutive of the state's self image. There was no stopping the tide, however. 'Changes in technology have fuelled a kind of backdoor liberalization and globalization of television ... DD no longer has a de facto monopoly over television' (Narayan 2014: 195).

By 1998, the first of India's private 24-hour news was on the air. 'No other country in the world had such a concentration of private news channels and the numbers are a stark illustration of the massive changes in Indian broadcasting, which until the early 1990s had remained a state monopoly' (Mehta 2014: 149). Private monopolies soon raised their head. By 2013, Vanita

Kohli-Khandekar was reporting that five networks—Star, Sony, Zee, Sun and Network18—controlled 65 per cent of all TV viewing in India (2013: 67). On the distribution side, six large direct-to-home operators controlled over 51 million homes. A handful of large players—Hathway, InCable, DEN Networks—were controlling the cable business.

So powerful were these interests that satellite broadcasting came to exist in a space almost free of regulatory impediment. The right to freedom of speech and expression was now interpreted to mean consuming the ad-fuelled programmes of satellite or cable television 24X7. There were, however, some attempts to control such advertising and programming driven by political imperatives. For instance, the BJP government, which had first come to power in 1998, wanted to be seen as promoting 'family values'. In 2000 it amended the Cable Act to ban the telecast of alcohol, tobacco and synthetic baby food ads; ensure that 'adult' content was telecast only between 11 PM and 6 AM, and prohibit advertising that injured religious sentiments. But the government collapsed, and so did the amendment.

Technically, the MIB still controlled the granting of licences for channel owners to operate in the country. First, the application of the applicant company must be found to be eligible. It is then sent for security clearance to the Ministry of Home Affairs while the MIB evaluates the suitability of the proposed channel for downlinking into India for public viewing. Once these clearances are achieved, a Grant of Permission Agreement is entered into by the applicant company and the MIB, after which the latter will issue a registration certificate allowing the concerned channel to broadcast. But all the bureaucratese involved in the process could not hide the reality that powerful enterprises, including those that presided over mainstream media empires, had come to own television channels and were aggressively influencing decisions taken by the State.

The history of Indian television is littered with policies put forward by the MIB that were soon quietly dropped. A Communications Convergence Bill in 2001, which proposed a Communications Commission of India to address overlaps in regulatory institutions, raised hackles because it came with an obligation to follow State directives. It was soon consigned to the back burner.

Then there was the Broadcast Bill of 2006 which sought to establish a Broadcast Regulatory Authority of India (BRAI), to facilitate and develop in an orderly manner the carriage and content of broadcasting for all forms of broadcasting, including cable, direct-to-home (DTH), radio services, satellite radio and so on. It wanted to restrict cross-media ownership 'to prevent monopolies and suggested caps on the total number of channels a company can have' (Kohli Khandekar 2013: 120).

But any such attempt to control cross-media ownership was tantamount to waving a red rag before powerful owners of multiple media outlets now seeking to expand their footprint in television. The Telecom Regulatory Authority of India (TRAI) was set up in 1997 to regulate telecom services, and one of its early attempts was to halt the threat of monopolies emerging in the media universe. Its report of August 2014 had argued that the growing trend of 'cross-media and vertical integration between TV broadcast and cable' needed to be arrested. It also recommended setting up an independent regulatory body to oversee both print and electronic media (Bhushan 2019: 54). Like the governments before it, the NDA-II government, which came to power in 2014, did not have the appetite to translate into policy these suggestions to curb cross-media ownership in television.

In order to stave off undue government interference and ensure their autonomy, some private broadcasters had hit upon an interesting stratagem in response to the criticism that television and radio did not have regulatory bodies like the Press Council of India or the Central Board of Film Certification. They proposed self-regulation. In 2007, the Broadcast Editors' Association (BEA) was set up with its own code of ethics, and a year later another group of 12 Indian broadcasters, operating 25 channels, came up, called the News Broadcasters Association (NBA), which later became the News Broadcasters & Digital Association (NBDA). These attempts were met with well-deserved cynicism. As media academic Sunetra Sen Narayan observed, the NBA did not represent all broadcasters and even their members flouted the norms that had been set (Narayan 2014: 220). 'Self-regulation', according to Prannoy Roy, one-time promoter of New Delhi Television Ltd (NDTV), gave television enormous 'soft power' to set the agenda. 'We have no real laws for defamation or libel, and no effective privacy laws. It is, frankly, a free-for-all environment ...' (Roy 2016: 14).

The Supreme Court also weighed in on the debate in August 2023, observing that while it agreed that regulation by the government could amount to pre-censorship or post-censorship, any self-regulatory mechanism had to be effective and that fines of up to Rs 1 lakh that the NBDA had been imposing could hardly work as a deterrent to inappropriate content.

That free-for-all environment Roy spoke about continues to the present day, and perhaps its most telling indicator is the battle among commercial television channels for Television Rating Points, or TRPs, in order to garner the all-important advertising rupee. The lack of a credible audience measurement system in the country, particularly since India has a large and multi-layered audience, has made for a free-for-all run with manipulated data being passed off as authentic profiling (*Economic Times* 2020).

The current sample size of 59,000 households utilised by the Broadcast Audience Research Council (BARC)—one of the larger television audience research entities—is laughable for a country with a viewership of well over a billion and with over 900 satellite television channels. The lack of a regulatory framework, which facilitated the growth of media in India, has been faithfully reflected in the chaotic policies that have marked audience measurement (Taneja 2024).

Plutocratic Upsurge

The NDA-II era saw new patterns of ownership emerge. Shortly after the BJP came to power in 2014, Reliance Industries Limited took over Network 18 Media and Investments Ltd in a classic 'marriage of the internet to existing capitalism', a term popularised by media academic Robert W. McChesney. With that one acquisition, India's biggest business house also became the country's largest media entity (Philipose 2019: 18). The phenomenon of 'owners, anchors, editors and managers, sometimes all rolled into one, driving news channels' (Bhushan 2019: 93) also came into being. A good example of this was the multilingual Republic TV, set up by Arnab Goswami.

By December 2022, Prannoy Roy himself ceded ownership of NDTV, one of the more credible television channels in the country, to the country's richest man at the time, Gautam Adani (*Mint* 2022). In a statement issued by the group shortly after the takeover, it was claimed that the interest of empowering 'Indian citizens, consumers and those interested in India, with information and knowledge' was what drove the deal. This grandiose principle was tested within a month of the acquisition. On 24 January 2023, Hindenburg Research, an American company specialising in financial research and short-selling stocks, published a report revealing that the Adani Group of companies was involved in stock manipulation and accounting fraud, but '[f]or three days, NDTV didn't touch the Hindenburg story. When it did, it carried Adani's statements verbatim, calling the revelations an "attack on India"' (Krishnan 2023).

It is against this backdrop that we need to revisit the 1995 Supreme Court verdict in *Cricket Association of Bengal and the Board of Control for Cricket in India (BCCI) v. Union of India*. It was arguably the country's most significant court verdict with regard to the administration of television, one that had special bearing on the constitutional guarantee of freedom of speech and expression. The case involved the attempt made by the MIB and Doordarshan to prevent Transworld International (TWI), a foreign sports television entity which had a contract to telecast the international Hero Cup cricket tournament being played in Kolkata, from exclusively telecasting the match, rather than recognising Doordarshan's right as the national broadcaster to also do so. Transworld International was accused of transgressing India's foreign exchange rules and it was even suggested that the Cricket Association of Bengal and the Board of Control for Cricket in India (BCCI) had betrayed the country's interests by preferring TWI to Doordarshan.

The question that the court grappled with was—who exactly owns the airwaves? Was it bureaucratic entities like Akashvani and Doordarshan/Prasar Bharti, which claimed to represent the people of India? Was it the market and various commercial interests that owned private channels? Or was it the Indian public?

Interestingly, the apex court refused to get locked into the familiar binary of government control versus that of commercial interests. It ruled that the airwaves, since they belong to all Indians, should be under the control of the public, as distinct from the government which represents the views and interests of the ruling party, or indeed the few private agencies of the rich that run broadcasting companies. As one of the judges put it,

> The airwaves and frequencies are public property. Their use has to be controlled and regulated by a public authority in the interests of the public, and to prevent the invasion of their rights. Since the electronic media involves the use of the airwaves, this factor creates an inbuilt restriction on its use, as in the case of any other public property.[6]

His colleague on the bench noted additionally that, since airwaves were public property, 'it is the duty of the State to see that airwaves are so utilized as to advance the free speech right of the citizens which is served by ensuring plurality and diversity of views, opinions and ideas'.[7]

In the process, the scope of the constitutional guarantee of freedom of speech and expression was enlarged to encompass the right to acquire and disseminate information and the right to communicate through any form of media, whether print, electronic or audiovisual.

As media academic Shanti Kumar noted,

> In defining the airwaves as a public property that is free from both state control and commercial forces, the judges were advancing a 'civic model' of public broadcasting where the public means community and citizenship, as distinct both from state sovereignty and market economy. (Kumar 2014: 87)

To this day, airwaves in India remain the duopoly which the 1995 Supreme Court verdict had hoped to bring to an end. Control over broadcasting continues to be vested in the government through the agency of a Prasar Bharti robbed of its autonomy, on the one hand, and, on the other, in the hands powerful private channels, many of whose owners control large cross-media empires. This, in turn, has severely undermined Article 19(1)(a) and its concomitant rights, described by a member of the Constituent Assembly at the dawn of India's freedom (Muralidharan 2018: 122) as the 'charter of our liberties.'

Notes

1. See the Rwanda Radio Transcripts, Montreal Institute for Genocide and Human Rights Studies.

2. See the Prasar Bharati (Broadcasting Corporation of India) Act, 1990.

3. For a summary of the recommendations made by both committees, see https://www.scribd.com/document/515797149/Joshi-Committee-and-Bachhawat-Committee (accessed February 2025).

4. Lok Sabha Unstarred Question (2000). Available at https://eparlib.nic.in/bitstream/123456789/392841/1/10732.pdf (accessed February 2025).

5. For an example of debates on the subject, see *Business Standard* (2015).

6. *The Secretary, Ministry Of … v. Cricket Association Of Bengal & Anr*, 1995. Available at https://indiankanoon.org/doc/539407/ (accessed February 2025).

7. *The Secretary, Ministry Of … v. Cricket Association Of Bengal & Anr*, 1995.

four

Freedom of Speech and Expression in the Digital Age

The internet is the culmination of nearly two centuries of electronic developments in communications.... [W]e are in a 'triple paradigm shift', wherein personal communication, mass media and market information have been subsumed with the new order so that the distinctions are becoming passé.

(McChesney 2013: 2–3)

While print, radio and television media took shape in the post-independence developmental phase of India's history, digital media grew in parallel with the emergence of economic liberalisation and globalisation. The foundational moment of digital computing in the country, however, can be traced to the developmental Nehruvian state and the post-independence drive to achieve self-sufficiency in electronics.

Among India's first computers was the HEC-2M, built in 1955 at the Indian Statistical Institute, Kolkata (Rajaraman 2015). Meanwhile work began at the Tata Institute of Fundamental Research in Mumbai on what was termed the 'automatic calculator'. The finished product was officially launched in 1960. Christened the 'Tata Institute of Fundamental Research Automatic Calculator' (TIFRAC), it was seen as an important step in providing the seedbed for national computation. Fifty years later, P. V. S. Rao, who was part of the team that assembled TIFRAC, recalled that the machine 'had a word length of 40 bits and a memory capacity of 1024 words' (Rao 2008: 425).

A few years later the Indian State launched its drive to manufacture computers in the country using local components. The Electronics Corporation of India Limited (ECIL) was set up in 1967 as a public sector unit under the Department of Atomic Energy to manufacture indigenous computer units. Two such units were manufactured, named TDC 312 and TDC 316, and they bore striking similarities to those manufactured in the US at that time. In 1976, even as the Indian citizen's right to freedom of expression was suspended during the Emergency, the Indira Gandhi government set up the National Informatics Centre to serve the computing needs of state bureaucracies and function as a repository of information at the national level. 'Informatics', or systems to process data for storage and retrieval, came to be perceived as vital to decision-making within government departments and ministries.

The US multinational IBM had around this time established a presence in India by selling refurbished American computers within the country. In 1977, the Janata government demanded that IBM set up an equity partnership with an Indian company and manufacture its computers locally. That policy move did not find favour with IBM, which wound up its operations here. The Janata government went ahead and privatised computer manufacturing in India the following year, leading to a few companies importing microprocessors in order to manufacture machines in India.

A computer policy which seeks to regulate the computer industry has a certain determinant, as Prabir Purkayastha noted, and that determinant is the role the government envisages for computers (1985: 72). Setting up ECIL was not dictated by any grandiose intention to deepen the citizen's right to freedom of speech and expression but rather the firm objective of the country to achieve self-reliance in electronics. The move to privatise computer manufacturing was also driven by a similar objective. Yet greater national self-reliance in electronics created the conditions for a larger number of people gaining access to more information.

The emphasis of successive governments thus far was on developing heavy engineering and human capacities to deliver on what Nehru once referred to as the 'temples of modern India'— large infrastructural projects like dams, steel making units, power plants and the like. Computerisation was seen as necessary only for those requirements that could not easily be achieved manually, like crunching very complex data sets for scientific and engineering requirements.

Changes in Computer Policy

This viewpoint was to change only in the 1980s, when the perception gained ground that large-scale computerisation was important for economic development. Policy-making soon came to reflect this. The Computer Policy, which had taken shape in the last days of the Indira Gandhi government, came into force after her son, Rajiv Gandhi, became prime minister in November 1984. This was followed by the Computer Software Export, Development and Training Policy of 1986. Both these strategic plans recognised software as an 'industry', which meant that the sector was now entitled to various incentives including subsidies and tax exemptions. By then planners had already made out a case for the marketisation of the computer sector by pointing out that India could enhance its presence in software production, given that there was a market of nearly Rs 10,000 crore for the computer industry within the country and software exports could bring in another Rs 1,000 crore (Purkayastha 1985).

The corporate media, impatient with the slow pace of the 'developmental model' and the 'Hindu rate of growth' hovering at around 3.5 per cent, emerged as strong advocates for economic liberalisation and globalisation and could not hide their excitement over this move. They glamourised Rajiv Gandhi and his ministers as 'computer boys' who were launching a modernisation project for the country based on computerisation. Business correspondent T. N. Ninan, in a magazine piece, held that this policy shift was particularly significant because, among all the counter-productive results of the government's industrial licensing and monitoring policies, the most ludicrous were in the burgeoning field of computers (Ninan 1984). His report was an enthusiastic endorsement of the move:

> Gone were the restrictive limitations on how much a computer manufacturing concern could produce, gone also were the high import duties on a variety of computers and components. And gone was the previous effort to keep a tight governmental control on what the industry did or didn't. (Ibid.)

Since these twin policies allowed the import of fully assembled motherboards with processors and reduced import duties, the emerging middle class could now look forward to buying cheaper computers, a point emphasised by one top corporate executive who informed the media that his group 'will certainly pass on the benefit of the duty reductions to the customer. The new policy will also help spread computerisation in the country' (ibid.).

Among India's first personal computers locally sold was the Neptune PC. A clone of models that were now available in the West, it was made available to the Indian consumer through a new enterprise that went by the name of Minicomp. Many other companies, including Wipro and DCM Data Products, joined the trail. Sales were sluggish initially because the prices of these devices—just short of a lakh—made them unaffordable to most consumers. It took a year or so, after the 1986 liberalisation kicked in, for Indian computers to become more affordable. Infotech analyst Sundeep Khanna (2021) points out that the numbers of units sold rose from 1,200 in 1985 to over 50,000 by 1989 and this softened prices as well.

In many ways, those first steps in the liberalisation of the information technology sector augured the formal liberalisation of the economy which was to take place in 1991 under Narasimha Rao's prime ministership. On the verge of defaulting on its foreign loans, India was obligated to meet the terms of the bail-out set by the International Monetary Fund (IMF), which included the opening up of the economy, the devaluation of the rupee and the marketisation of the economy. All this created a large cohort of consumers with disposable income. Encouragement to the information technology (IT) sector drove and was driven by the need to leverage communication outreach for monetary ends. Several steps undertaken by the government followed. Computers could now be more easily imported with tax breaks and lowered duties, and regulations on foreign collaborations were pared down. Nothing captured the impacts of this phase better than the fact that, between 1991 and 1997, the software services industry grew at an annual growth rate exceeding 30 per cent, even as economic growth, which had hovered around 3.8 per cent from 1950 to 1990, suddenly shot up to around 7 per cent within two years of liberalisation (Rajaraman 2015).

Not everyone was invited to the party, however. To get an idea of the disparities in access, a look at the figures thrown up by the 2011 national census—the very first time that there was an attempt by the Indian State to capture the big picture of computer use on a pan-national scale—may be useful. It pointed to just 9.4 per cent of households in the country having either a laptop or a computer, with only 3 per cent of these homes also having an Internet connection. While 20 per cent of urban households and 5 per cent of rural households owned a computer or laptop, only 1 per cent of rural Indian households owned a computer and an internet connection. Further disparities emerge. Only 6.5 per cent of Scheduled Caste homes owned a computer/laptop, while for tribal families the figure came down to 5.2 per cent (Bhagat 2018). There was no data on access to computers along gender lines. However, we can surmise that the gender gap was formidable if we look at the data on rural education thrown up in a survey conducted in 2017 which showed that, while 49 per cent of rural males had never used the internet, close to 76 per cent of females had never done so (Annual Status of Education Report [Rural] 2017).

Undoubtedly, it was the urban middle class, largely upper-caste, male and professionalised, which was best placed to benefit from the early policies on computerisation and software development. The emphasis on tertiary education adopted by successive post-independence governments, right from the days of Nehru, meant that by 2010, as pioneering computer educationist V. Rajaraman observed, 1.3 million engineers were graduating in India every year, with 32 per cent of them specialising in computer engineering and infotech. While the graduating students were not uniformly well-trained, the graduates of the IITs and NITs (around 10,000) were outstanding. It was the latter cohort of English-speaking professionals who could benefit from training programmes in the country and abroad (Rajaraman 2015), and who then went on to leverage their skills in computer programming and software design, both within India and across the world. The outsourcing of service-sector jobs to India from the West was seen by academics like Leela Fernandes as a process which 'consolidated the structural basis of India's rising new middle class' (2006: 114).

An argument could be made that the rapid liberalisation of the IT sector was a major factor in creating deep disparities which marked Indian society then, and continues to do so. Yet the everyday conveniences of computerisation and IT did percolate to large sections of the population and benefited many. The success of the computerised ticket reservation system of the Indian Railways in 1976, for instance, put an end to the long queues outside railway counters and reduced ticketing scams. The ATM machine, introduced in a private bank a year later, soon became an indispensable part of banking services for the middle classes.

The political consensus between successive governments on the need to keep liberalising the telecom sector—a policy sentiment that, as we saw, had first manifested in the 1980s—continued over the following decades. It came to represent the touchstone of economic liberalisation in the country. The BJP government led by Atal Bihari Vajpayee in 1999 ended the State monopoly over telecom. The Telecom Policy that was set into motion introduced a new revenue-sharing model, which in turn drove down the prices of both mobile phones and call rates. Such a move was calculated to stoke the 'international ambitions of the software industry' (Athique 2012: 68). In 2007, Prime Minister Manmohan Singh publicly declared that 'growth in the telecom sector is a critical component of our infrastructure plans and it plays an important catalytic role in our development process. The opening up of the telecom sector has created an impressive forward momentum in India....'[1]

The markets responded enthusiastically to these efforts. By 2002, mobile phone ownership in India had overtaken fixed connections, allowing large sections of the population to leapfrog the landline technology phase that they had never used, or could never have used, given its unaffordability. Fuelling the exponential growth of the mobile phone in India were several other factors, including a telling rise in average incomes, especially those of the middle classes, along with plummeting user costs of mobile use. Robin Jeffrey and Assa Doron (2013: 6) point out that India, given the high volumes of use it generated, could develop the cheapest mobile call rates in the world.

Just as the decision to broadcast the Asian Games in colour in the early 1980s, with State-run Doordarshan using INSAT 1A, had intended and unintended consequences in terms of creating a new communication infrastructure, which in turn expanded freedom of speech and expression by improving access to information, the mobile phone and later the internet by the turn of the twenty-first century were creating new patterns of life and deepening access to information.

Impact of the Internet

The internet, much like early television presence in India—which was made possible through the initiative of the US government, as we saw in Chapter 3—was facilitated in 1986 by the United Nations Development Programme (UNDP) in partnership with the Indian government, as a research network for scholars. A couple of years later, the National Informatics Centre began to operate Nicnet, designed to enhance communication links between government departments. It was only in the next decade that it was made accessible to the wider Indian public. This major move came on Independence Day, 1995, and the symbolism was not lost: one newspaper carried the headline 'Independence Day to mean freedom with the Internet'. Internet services were offered initially through the sole agency of the government-run telecom company, Videsh Sanchar Nigam Ltd (VSNL), and within six months, it was reporting a client base of 10,000 (*Mint* 2015). It was another matter, as we saw, that this freedom initially benefitted those individuals who were more likely than not to be prosperous, urban-based, upper-caste, English-speaking and male, given the prohibitively high cost of access.

The picture was to change drastically in the decade that followed. The telecom sector was opened up to competitive bidding from private players along with considerable investment directed at building infrastructure, much of which also came from private sources. In the first decade of the twenty-first century alone, 'the telecom sector has received on average 8.2 per cent of total inward FDI between 2000–01 and 2010–11' (Telecom Regulatory Authority of India 2012) and most of these inflows went into the cellular mobile segment. This was a pattern that stablised over time. By December 2022, the telecom sector was the third largest sector in India in terms of FDI inflow, contributing 6.43 per cent of total FDI inflow (Telecom Regulatory Authority of India 2023).

Liberalisation of the telecom sector saw mobile tariffs in India decline steeply to become among the cheapest in the world and suddenly affordable to the working poor. A boom in the local manufacture of cell phones drove their prices down. What made mobile use even cheaper were innovative practices. There was what came to be known as the 'Budget Telecom Network Model', which emerged in the South Asian markets of India, Pakistan and Bangladesh to cater to 'customers who only use a few calling minutes per month'. Telecom corporates like Bharti Airtel cashed in on this model by introducing as far back as 1999 a pre-paid cell phone card called 'Magic', which could be acquired for an affordable price. In addition, there were user innovations such as the deployment of the missed call, which did the job of signalling a message without the user having to actually pay for a call. Being 'connected' was now no longer a luxury—it became a vital cog in the business of earning a livelihood. Jeffrey and Doron cited a survey of small businesses in a few cities in 2008 that found 11 different occupations relying on the mobile phone. This included a labour exchange for manual workers (2013: 116).

The mobile phone was soon to prove a gateway to greater internet access. In 2010, with the coming of 3G services, the compact between the internet and the Indian—still largely upper-class, upper-caste, male and urban—deepened, with the internet now being accessed on mobile devices. The next year, the Manmohan Singh government came up with a draft of yet another National Telecom Policy which envisaged 'broadband on demand' by the year 2015. The aim was to achieve 175 million broadband connections by 2017 and 600 million by 2020 at a minimum download speed of two megabits per second. It also envisioned broadening internet access in rural areas through high-speed and high-quality broadband access to all village panchayats through optical fibre by the year 2014 and progressively to all villages and habitations.

Over the first decade and a half of the twenty-first century, the growth rate of internet use in India was astronomical, largely because of mobile-enabled internet services. The irony was that while the majority of Indians did not own computers or landline telephones, they would never have to do so, thanks to the smartphone. It led at least one commentator to hail the internet-enabled smartphone as the 'greatest national upheaval since Partition' (Agarwal 2018: 17). While this may seem technologically deterministic, one cannot deny the decisive role mobile technology came to play in people's lives, although many of these changes were mired in strident accusations of corruption which, ironically, led to the politicians and policy-makers themselves being consigned to the dustbin of history. Allegations of graft and profiteering, especially within the telecom sector, were a major factor for the

Congress-led government being swept away from power in the 2014 general election.

New communications technologies—new media and social media taken together—marked a paradigm shift in expanding the definition of what was termed 'media', which was thus far taken to mean print, radio and television. They brought about changes in usage patterns, since human interactivity was intrinsic to their use. They had, besides, 'speed, simulation, connectivity, convergence, and mobility and to coin a new term "instantaneity", meaning the quick response facilitated by new media, especially visible in social media' (Narayan and Narayanan 2016: 10).

This mélange of internet-mediated communication tools and practices has undoubtedly deepened people's right to freedom of speech and expression. Manuel Castells argues that 'horizontal networks make possible the rise of ... mass self-communication, decisively increasing the autonomy of communicating subjects vis-à-vis communication corporations, as the users become both senders and receivers of messages' (Castells 2013: 4). Such exchange of information enhances knowledge and sociality, creates opinion, furthers business and trade and builds common understanding and solidarities.

The question then is this: Do such new communication tools alter the nature of the right to freedom of speech and expression? Legal theorist Jack M. Balkin argues that while digital technologies do not fundamentally alter the concept of freedom of speech, 'they change the social conditions in which people speak, and by changing the social conditions of speech, they bring to light features of freedom of speech that have always existed in the background but now become foregrounded' (Balkin 2004: 2). These social conditions are basically what was also emphasised by Castells (2013) when he noted widespread cultural participation and interaction that previously could not have existed on the same scale.

First Attempts to Control Digital Speech

Given the scale of their potential impact, digital technologies are also susceptible to being severely constrained or captured by various entities, whether they are gargantuan digital corporations or authoritarian governments.

One of the first cases that highlighted the potential impacts of digital media was the SMS campaign calling for 'Justice for Jessica' in 2005 (Srivastava and Roy 2016: 27). Before long, the Indian State felt the need to shore up its powers to control digital communication given the unprecedented extent to which information could now permeate the public sphere.

With newer technologies unleashing the self-communication of large sections of the population came ever fresher challenges for the State. The first government to seriously legislate on digital media was the Atal Bihari Vajpayee government during its second term, which extended from 1999 to 2004. It brought in two significant pieces of legislation—the Information Technology Act, 2000 and the Communication Convergence Bill, 2001.

The second never made it into the statute books but its intent to control the digital sphere demonstrated impressive political ambition. Recognising that the era of the internet had created a convergence of media technologies, it set out to achieve two transformations through a single Bill. *First*, to repeal legislation that was regulating this space thus far, including the colonial Indian Telegraph Act, 1885, the Indian Wireless Telegraphy Act, 1933 and post-independence enactments like the Telegraph Wires (Unlawful Possession) Act, 1950, the Telecom Regulatory

Authority of India Act, 1997 and the Cable Television Networks (Regulation) Act, 1995. *Second*, to replace the old regulatory apparatus with a government-appointed super-regulator armed with a broad spectrum of powers, to handle all aspects of the digital sphere, including their carriage (equipment/devices) and their content. It was also to be invested with dispute resolution functions. The Bill came up against strong objections from a slew of stakeholders, including trade bodies and media experts, which led to it being put on the backburner. Two decades later, some of these legislative proposals were again revived by another BJP government, this time under Narendra Modi's premiership, as we shall see later in this chapter.

In contrast, the Information Technology Act, 2000—the first move that the Government of India had ever made to assert its jurisdiction over the digital space—was up and running without any controversy. Passed in June 2000 by the Vajpayee government, at the dawn of the twenty-first century, the law went on to cast a long shadow on the years that followed. Although it was a pioneering piece of legislation, it made no references to the digital rights of the citizen. In that sense, a piece of legislation that claimed to be a 'model law' missed out on an opportunity to interpret Article 19(1)(a) for the digital age.

Its central focus, instead, was ostensibly on regulating 'electronic commerce', securing electronic records and preventing online fraud. But Section 67 of the Act abruptly switches to prescribing punishment for the purveying of online pornographic material, indicating that the government also wished to use the new law to regulate information. A Cyber Appellate Tribunal—later termed the Cyber Regulations Appellate Tribunal—was the chief governing body for the law and the central government notified all relevant cybersecurity breaches to this body. The point to note here is that this powerful tribunal was directly appointed by the central government.

While the Information Technology Act, 2000, as we have already noted, did not concern itself with the digital rights of users, what made it far more intrusive was a slew of amendments introduced by the UPA government in December 2008. The fraught atmosphere prevailing in the country following the Mumbai attacks of November that year ensured that the changes made could pass through both Houses of Parliament, without discussion or even cursory scrutiny, and come into force the following year. According to a newspaper report (*The Telegraph Online* 2015), one of the sections introduced—66A—was moved for passage in exactly 21 minutes!

That Section, 66A, was in fact so broad in its definitions that it was almost a reversal of the constitutional guarantee of free speech. Users of a 'computer resource or a communication device' could be punished for 'sending offensive messages'. The astonishing list of offending use cases includes sharing information that the sender knows to be false for the purpose of 'causing annoyance, inconvenience, danger, obstruction, insult, injury, criminal intimidation, enmity, hatred or ill will, persistently....' Nowhere in the amendment were words like 'annoyance', 'inconvenience', 'danger' and so on defined, despite the punishment they attracted being significant. Violations could invite a prison term of up to three years, while another amended section, 66F, had provisions for what was labelled 'cyber terrorism', which could invite a life term.

Also introduced was Section 69, which gave the government the power to issue directions for interception, monitoring or decryption of any information through any computer resource, if the Centre or state governments, or any of their officers, were 'satisfied that it is necessary or expedient so to do, in the interest of the sovereignty or integrity of India, defence of India, security of the State, friendly relations with foreign States or public order....' It also gave the government the power to block public access to any information and the power to monitor and collect traffic data or information through any computer resource for cyber security. The government was also granted the power to 'issue directions to authorize any agency to monitor and collect traffic data or information through any computer resource for cyber security'.

Intermediaries—defined as 'any person or entity who on behalf of another person receives, stores, or transmits that electronic record or provides any service with respect to that record'—were not liable under the Act for any information put out by a third party, provided they did not modify such information. However, an intermediary could face action for any violation, including failure to expeditiously remove material deemed objectionable by the government.

All aspects of the functioning of the Act were now to be overseen by the Indian Computer Emergency Response Team. It must be noted that this body, along with the Cyber Regulations Appellate Tribunal set up under the original Act, which together provide the regulatory muscle to check infringements of the IT Act, lacked independence since both were appointed by the government.

The 2008 amendments were followed in 2009 by the Information Technology (Procedure and Safeguards for Blocking for Access of Information by Public) Rules, and in 2011 by the Information Technology (Reasonable Security Practices and Procedures and Sensitive Personal Data or Information) Rules, 2011, both of which defined the bureaucratic regime under which digital communication and media would need to function. The system for the interception, monitoring and decryption of information was to be set up and overseen by the 'competent authority', which had the heavy hand of government writ all over it.

The proliferation of new digital technologies and a sharp rise in cyber crime, including sexual offences, certainly demanded enlightened legislation. The concern was that the IT Act, 2000, and the amendments, orders and policies that followed over the next two decades and more, constituted a system that enabled government control over citizens' right to free speech and expression. The legislative architecture created in the process allowed the State to acquire draconian, unprecedented and unaccountable powers of monitoring, blocking and general surveillance which potentially threatened individual rights and, in the long run, undermined the very essence of Indian democracy. In fact it has been observed that the 2008 amendments were 'far more intrusive than the Indian Telegraph Act of 1885, which was drafted to protect the interests of the British Raj' (cited in Gupta 2010: 45).

A pathway for greater state control over the digital space was thus created. In December 2011, amidst the India Against Corruption campaign, the UPA government tested the newly refurbished IT Act by asking IT behemoths including Facebook, Google and Microsoft to come up with a framework to 'pre-screen' data before it was uploaded on their websites (Timmons 2011). It was careful to state that this was not to be seen as a move to censor freedom of expression on the internet but as one designed to protect Indian citizens from 'offensive' material making its way to popular social media sites. The concerned companies resisted the government's move by stating that they were governed by community standards prevailing in the US. Given the blowback from the US corporate establishment, the move was quietly dropped but such tussles were to become more commonplace in the years that followed.

Meanwhile, the police made full use of the amended provisions of the IT Act, 2000, as testified to by innumerable cases filed subsequently. In the year 2012 alone, governments and police authorities in various parts of the country resorted to Section 66A in an almost cavalier manner. At least six prominent cases were to surface. In April that year a Jadavpur University professor, who had incurred the wrath of the chief minister of West Bengal for sharing on social media a cartoon which showed her in a bad light, faced arrest. It took him over 10 years of litigation to get the case dismissed (*The Indian Express* 2023). In May, two members of Air India's cabin crew were jailed for 12 days for circulating online already published jokes about politicians, including the prime minister, and insulting the national flag (*The Hindu* 2012). In September there was the well-publicised case involving a young cartoonist, Aseem Trivedi, who was imprisoned under various laws, including 66A, for a cartoon that appeared on his website and Facebook page, which trenchantly critiqued the Indian Parliament (*The Indian Express* 2012). That November, a young Palghar-based woman, Shaheen Dadha, posted a comment on Mumbai having shut down over the death of Bal Thackeray, Shiv Sena founder. She ended her post with the comment, 'Today Mumbai shuts down due to fear, not due to respect.' Not only was she arrested, a friend of hers, Rinu Srinivasan, who had 'liked' her post, was also taken into custody (Salunke 2015). That same month, in another part of country, the Puducherry police swooped down on a small-time businessman for tweeting critically about the finances of the son of the then Union finance minister, P. Chidambaram (Agarwal and Rustagi 2012). The year ended with yet another arbitrary and outrageous 66A action, when a youth who sent a birthday cake to the home of a friend of his that carried a picture of hers taken from her Facebook page had an FIR filed against him by her parents for the unauthorised use of the image.

State surveillance, enabled by the amendments and orders, now became more evident. In 2013, Google in its transparency report of April, revealed that the Indian government's take-down requests had nearly doubled in number in the second half of 2012 in comparison to the first half of that year (*The Hindu* 2013). The trend was to continue even as the new government under Narendra Modi came to power in 2014. Facebook's Transparency Report for the first six months of 2015 revealed that the NDA-II government had asked for more than 15,000 items to be removed from its site (Srivastava and Roy 2016: 36) for various reasons ranging from hate speech to incitement of religious violence and defamation.

Cases Fought for Digital Rights

The national outrage provoked by the manner in which Section 66A was being instrumentalised by the State and its coercive apparatus led to several writ petitions being filed in various courts against it. One, pertaining to the arrests of the two Palghar women for their Facebook posts, argued for the section to be declared ultra vires and came up in the Supreme Court before a bench presided over by Chief Justice Altamas Kabir and Justice J. Chelameswar. The judges observed, 'The way the children were arrested and treated like criminals outraged the conscience of a major section of society' (*UdayIndia* 2013). In response to the adverse remarks of the justices, and their observation that 66A was far too wide, the GOI in a pre-emptive move issued an advisory to the police that before any arrests were made under this section, it would first have to be cleared by an officer of a rank not below that of Inspector General of Police/Deputy Commissioner or Superintendent of Police. The offending section, however, remained intact.

This formed the backdrop to the *Shreya Singhal v. Union of India* case of 2015. Juridical theorist Gautam Bhatia termed it 'a soaring judgment that dwelt upon the foundational importance of free speech in a pluralist democracy' (Bhatia 2019: 251). It could be termed one of a crucially important triumvirate of apex court verdicts on digital rights and freedoms. The second, delivered in 2018—*Justice K. S. Puttaswamy (Retd) v. Union of India*—underlined the foundational value of privacy in the digital age, an aspect that we will consider in some detail later. Finally, there was the verdict of *Anuradha Bhasin v. Union of India*, 2020, which examined whether internet shutdowns undermined the right to freedom of speech and expression, in the context of the long suspension of the internet during and after the abrogation of Article 370 in Jammu and Kashmir in August 2019. The verdict recognised that access to the internet was a basic human right[2] and that the right to free speech and the right to carry out trade and business through the internet are protected by the Indian Constitution. However, that judgment also cited exceptions to Article 19 (1)(a) that empower the State to impose reasonable restrictions in appropriate cases.

Let us briefly return to the first of these momentous apex court pronouncements. The *Shreya Singhal* petitions brought before the Supreme Court by lawyer Shreya Singhal, et al., challenged Section 66 A of the IT Act, 2000, and Section 69A, both included in the law by the 2008 amendments. They argued that various sections of the Indian Penal Code (IPC) were sufficient to address the crimes these amendments sought to address.

In its response to this case, the court recognised three concepts which it saw as fundamental in understanding the reach of this most basic of human rights, that is, right to freedom of speech and expression. The first is discussion, the second is advocacy and the third is incitement: 'Mere discussion or even advocacy of a particular cause howsoever unpopular is at the heart of Article 19(1)(a). It is only when such discussion or advocacy reaches the level of incitement that Article 19(2) kicks in.'[3]

The petitioners had argued that the net cast by Section 66A was very wide and therefore violated the public's right to information. The court concurred with this view:

> The petitioners are right in saying that Section 66A in creating an offence against persons who use the internet and annoy or cause inconvenience to others very clearly affects the freedom of speech and expression of the citizenry of India at large in that such speech or expression is directly curbed by the creation of the offence contained in Section 66A.[4]

There is a significant discussion in the judgment on what constitutes 'reasonable restriction' with regard to Article 19(2), with the court noting that the word 'reasonable' implies intelligent care and deliberation and that legislation which arbitrarily or excessively invades the right cannot be said to be 'reasonable'. Similarly, the court strikingly pointed out that the right to freedom of speech and expression included the right to disseminate information to as wide a section of the population as was possible, something that was facilitated by the electronic media. Therefore, it was argued, the 'virtues of the electronic media cannot become its enemies'.[5]

The court took note of the fact that, because the section was vague and overly broad, it had resulted in several instances of innocents being made to suffer because of it. This, it observed, is really an 'insidious form of censorship which impairs a core value contained in Article 19(1)(a)', and which would have a chilling effect on the freedom of speech and expression. In the face of all this, the court had no hesitation in striking it down as violative of Article 19(1)(a), even as it recognised that speech on the internet was distinct from speech in the media of print or broadcast or live speech, because it gave individuals a platform with a low threshold of entry to air their views. Section 69A, however, was allowed to remain because it was a more 'narrowly drawn provision with safeguards'.

The interesting aspect of Section 66A is that it had a long afterlife and continued to impede the right of citizens to freedom of speech and expression. The police persisted in applying it even years after the apex court's ruling, indicating what a useful handle it was for State repression. In July 2021, the People's Union of Civil Liberties (PUCL) petitioned the Supreme Court, citing cases running into hundreds that were continuing to be filed under Section 66A despite the apex court having struck it down (Mahapatra 2021).

Welfare Delivery Goes Online

The NDA-II government was in its second year when the *Shreya Singhal* verdict was pronounced, prompting the government to go back to the drawing board with Section 66A. A high-level committee was appointed to evolve an instrument that would 'deal with national security issues and what steps can be taken to accommodate all the concerns in the absence of Section 66A' (*Hindustan Times* 2015). Various iterations of the draft legislation related to this were to emerge in the years that followed, which we will examine later.

Among Narendra Modi's first policies on becoming prime minister was to adopt several of the digital initiatives that the previous Manmohan Singh government had set up and place his government's stamp on them. An instance of this was the use of the digitised biometric identification system known as Aadhaar, which allots a 12-digit unique identification number to each individual and is linked to their biometric and demographic data. Despite Modi having attacked the idea as wasteful during his 2014 election campaign, he made it a foundational accessory to his welfare measures (*The Hindu Businessline* 2018). In 2015, he converted the National e-Governance Plan of the previous regime into the 'Digital India Programme'. India was to be transformed into a 'digitally empowered society and knowledge economy'[6] based on what was described as three vision areas: digital infrastructure as a core utility to every citizen; governance and services on demand; and digital empowerment of citizens.

Direct benefit transfer of money through digital means—first launched in January 2013—had by 2015 become part of the Modi government's fully digitalised welfare agenda through the 2015 Pradhan Mantri Jan Dhan Yojana (PMJDY). Pared-down banking accounts to individuals above the age of 10 across India were made available through the PMJDY, with the total beneficiaries, according to government figures for February 2025, now over 500 million. The emphasis on digitalisation for welfare delivery came under the nifty acronym JAM—Jan Dhan-Aadhaar-Mobile. In addition, there was the Unified Payments Interface (UPI), a pan-national digital payments ecosystem. It has been said that the 'combination of Aadhaar, PMJDY, and a surge in mobile communication has reshaped the way citizens access government services' (Draboo 2020). Together these digital initiatives enabled greater inclusion of those who were earlier left out of the country's financial system and government services at a pan-national level and, it also could be said, expanded their right to information and expression. Variations on this model were introduced during the years of the COVID-19 pandemic, as for instance through CoWin, a digital platform which was widely used to roll out and monitor vaccine distribution in 2020–2021.

This extensive reliance on the use of digitalisation for welfare delivery, while being hailed for the conveniences it provided, also raised legitimate fears of mass State and corporate surveillance. Data theft and incursions into privacy were also to emerge as major concerns, as did the fact that many digitally disempowered people, including the elderly with worn-out fingerprints, found themselves left out of the frame.

Digital Disempowerment

Undoubtedly digital technologies have enabled Indians to access new routes to information and inclusion, but there was a major paradox. Digitalisation in the country, which was meant to empower digital citizens, appears to be driven by several interests, most of them not immediately visible to those who use them. This leaves them open to potential sources of disempowerment. Daya Kishan Thussu points to 'an interesting synergy emerging: an unabashedly pro-business government of Narendra Modi with its "Digital India" programmes is strongly supported by hugely influential domestic corporations (Reliance's Jio is a case in point), as well as global digital corporations (Google, Facebook and Microsoft—to name the most prominent ones)' (Thussu 2016: viii).

As digital giants tighten their hold on the digitalisation process, there is simultaneously an intensification of the digital divide across class, gender, demographic and caste lines. More men than women, to take one example, had active accounts by virtue of the fact that more of them owned mobile handsets and had access to the internet. There were also the deleterious effects of other asymmetries as well. Among the digital behemoths, Facebook— an early optimiser of India's digitalisation—benefitted directly from affordable mobile data in innumerable ways. In 2022, the triumvirate of Facebook, WhatsApp (acquired by Meta to exploit its strong India-centric user base in April 2014 for US $19 million) and Instagram—all owned by Facebook/Meta—figured among the top three 'Most Used Platforms' in India.[7] This has allowed these platforms to be instrumentalised, both by private interests for corporate aggrandisement and by political parties to extend their reach and clinch electoral victories.

A digital ecosphere rife with disinformation has potentially severely disempowering consequences for ordinary Indians. Periods of crisis see an intensification of such disinformation. During the pandemic of 2020–2021, social media was awash with fake therapies offered as cures, including cow urine as a remedy for COVID-19. Joyojeet Pal and Syeda Zainab Akbar (2020) suggest that the misinformation ecology has a spectrum of malicious intent, 'including ill-informed claims, clickbait headlines, news out of context, manipulation, and outright fabrication. Of these, the first, rooted in ignorance or what scholarship refers to as belief perseverance, and the last—intentional disinformation, are likely to cross our paths on a daily basis.'

The important question that media theorist Robert McChesney raises in his book, *Digital Disconnect, How Capitalism is Turning the Internet Against Democracy*, is this: 'in view of the Internet's magnitude, complexity, exponential growth, and unpredictable gyrations, how can we even begin to make sense of what is taking place?' (2013: 3) The age of digitalisation has witnessed several social dissonances, including rising dependency on mobile phones that verges on addiction, and the general creation of cognitive dysfunction arising out of social disconnect. The anonymity and instantaneity that the internet provides have given fraudsters, trolls and online stalkers a free rein. Crimes against women have taken on new avatars in cyberspace, ranging from non-consensual and 'revenge' pornography, digital voyeurism and child pornography to cyber obscenity. Legislative instruments to tackle these crimes are 'half baked' and therefore ineffectual, according to criminologists (Halder and Jaishankar 2017).

New threats to well-being hitherto unknown to humans have emerged, like deepfakes where images, video or audio recordings are edited using artificial intelligence in a way that invests the original subjects with someone else's personal attributes. Since they appear authentic, they have serious real-life consequences. The example is often cited of a deepfake video which depicted V. Zelenskyy, president of Ukraine, calling upon his troops to surrender shortly after the Russian invasion of the country in 2022 and which could have jeopardised Ukraine's ability to defend itself (Yasar, Barney and Wigmore 2023). While deepfakes have a legitimate role in gaming equipment or in services such as forwarding calls and voice restoring treatment, they can have extremely dangerous consequences due to their effectiveness in spreading false information. This is especially dangerous in a society like India, which is marked by deep inequalities in literacy and where people do not have what media academic Hany Farid termed a 'shared factual system'. It is in such information vacuums that authoritarianism emerges, he argued (*The Times of India* 2023).

Women are particularly vulnerable to such gross image manipulation. US-based singer Taylor Swift is believed to be the person most frequently targeted with deepfakes in the world, and in early 2024, pornographic visuals of her persona went viral on X, attracting millions of views. India too has seen a similar weaponising of the technology. In 2023, popular actress Rashmika Mandanna had the distressing experience of having a video, supposedly of her entering a lift in a bodysuit, go viral. The deepfake was based on a video featuring influencer Zara Patel and was generated using technology which is today widely available, making it harder to pinpoint the source even as it becomes increasingly easy to generate such content (Jaiman 2023). The motivations for those who create deepfakes may vary. In the Mandanna case, the creator was driven allegedly by the desire to increase viewership of a fan page he was running in her name.

Freedom of speech and expression, if it is not to descend into a dystopia of fake images and information designed to manipulate minds, has to be founded on authentic information. But addressing deepfakes has to begin with checking the abuse of surveillance technologies and increasing social media literacy so that morphed images can be identified. Above all, it requires enabling the flow of authentic information through right to information mechanisms and public education. Curbing deepfakes post-facto through criminal legislation and blanket censorship, which is what governments tend to do, may have the contrary effect of keeping the population trapped in a web of surveillance and disinformation.

Importance of Privacy in the Digital Age

Undergirding many of these digital harms is the loss of individual privacy, which will only become manifest as AI comes to dominate the digital space. The seriousness of this threat has rarely been publicly articulated or legislated upon in India. While the framers of the Constitution saw the importance of freedom of speech and expression for post-independence India, there was little recognition that these freedoms were crucially dependent on the right to privacy. Gautam Bhatia, in his book *The Transformative Constitution* (2019), points out that, during the Constituent Assembly debates, a provision safeguarding the privacy of correspondence, put forward by Somnath Lahiri, was rejected.

Lahiri's colleagues Kazi Syed Karimuddin and Pandit Thakur Das Bhargava tried to reinsert it into the constitutional text but without success, despite Ambedkar's endorsement. That was how the 'constitution came into being without an express fundamental right to privacy' (Bhatia 2019: 219).

The digital era, with its invasive technologies like facial recognition systems and the emergence of the surveillance State, led to what, as has already been noted, was one of three most important Supreme Court verdicts of the digital era—*K. S. Puttaswamy (Retd) v. Union of India*, 2017. On 24 August 2017, a nine-judge constitution bench read out their unanimous opinion that informational privacy was an important aspect of the right to privacy, and that the right to privacy was intrinsic to Article 21 of the Constitution, which protects life and liberty.

> Informational privacy is a facet of the right to privacy. The dangers to privacy in an age of information can originate not only from the state but from non-state actors as well. We commend to the Union Government the need to examine and put into place a robust regime for data protection.[8]

A development a year after this crucial verdict signals the NDA-II government's intent to tamp down the impact of the *Puttaswamy* verdict. On 20 December 2018, the Union home minister issued a wide-ranging order providing sweeping powers to intelligence, tax and law enforcement agencies to 'intercept, monitor and decrypt any information generated, transmitted, received or stored in any computer' (*The Times of India* 2018). Although the government claimed that the order was only a reiteration of existing rules, and the move was only to gather intelligence to address national security concerns, it raised anxieties that the real targets of such surveillance would be opposition leaders, mediapersons as well as dissenters/human rights defenders.

Shackling Digital Media Actors

From 2017 through the pandemic years, ministers in the NDA-II Cabinet, notably Smriti Irani during her short term as Union information and broadcasting minister between 2017 and 2018, kept exploring ways to control digital news. The reasons they cited ranged from the need to check the proliferation of 'fake news' to stopping content that went against Indian culture, including pornography. Most of these early attempts were fiercely resisted by various stakeholders, including members of the public.

After Narendra Modi won the 2019 general election and became prime minister for the second time, efforts on this front were redoubled. While FDI for print media and television media purveying news and current affairs was capped at 26 per cent and 49 per cent respectively, there had been thus far no cap on FDI in the digital media space. In 2019, new rules were introduced that capped FDI for digital media at 26 per cent, and made government approval a necessary condition for such investment. This was immediately perceived by digital media observers as arbitrary and restrictive (*The Hindu Businessline* 2021). Additionally, in the same year, the Right to Information (Amendment) Act came into force, which diluted the status of information commissioners and thereby their independence. The RTI law, which was passed in 2005, has proved to be an important tool for investigative journalism, and mediapersons have a direct stake in its efficacy. Therefore, efforts to dilute its impact have direct implications for freedom of speech.

On 25 February 2021, Union Minister of Electronics and Information Technology Ravi Shankar Prasad and Union Minister of Information and Broadcasting Prakash Javadekar jointly unveiled the Information Technology (Intermediary Guidelines and Digital Ethics Code) Rules, 2021. Drawing their legitimacy from sections of the Information Technology Act, 2000, and the Information

Technology (Intermediaries Guidelines) Rules, 2011, the rules sought to address public concern over issues like fake news, child pornography, online gaming and the possible compromise of national integrity and security. This despite the fact that there are general laws already in existence to tackle such concerns.

The IT Rules, which the ministers described as a 'soft touch oversight mechanism', demanded self-regulation on the part of digital players. In actual fact, what was being demanded was pliancy. Mandatory self-censorship was built into a three-tiered architecture of the grievance redressal pyramid, with the government heading it through its 'oversight mechanism' and powers to order content to be taken down. Digital entities are required to 'acknowledge' any complaints made by any individual within 24 hours and resolve such complaints within a period of 15 days. If a complaint is not acted upon, the individual making the complaint can appeal to the government-appointed Grievance Appellate Committee, which will 'endeavour to resolve the appeal finally within thirty calendar days from the date of receipt of the appeal'.

One of the most disturbing aspects of this formulation was that it enabled lateral surveillance of the public. From where, after all, would the 'grievances' come? They would emerge from 'interested' parties and could even be manufactured to extend political and personal agendas. A distinct characteristic of the Modi era has been the emergence of peer-to-peer monitoring for ideological purposes. It was the foundation on which the vigilante activism was based and which saw the rise of lynchings of supposed beef eaters and rising assaults on inter-faith couples accused of 'love jihad'. This model is now being transplanted on to the media space, leading to great disruption (Philipose 2021).

Although cases were filed against the new rules, what was striking was that, despite adverse rulings and observations from UN Special Rapporteurs that these rules 'do not meet the requirements of international law and standards related to the rights to privacy and freedom of expression, as protected by the International Covenant on Civil and Political Rights, which India acceded to in 1979' (*Livelaw.in* 2021), the government was in no way deterred from going ahead with them. What is more, several amendments were made to enhance the State's capacity to control social and internet media and several of its features—including the elaborate grievance redressal architecture it envisaged—were replicated in rules, orders and laws passed subsequently.

In its earliest iteration, the rules only set down the obligation on the part of social media intermediaries to inform users of the new regulations. A year and a half later, amendments were made to the IT Rules which required intermediaries to publicise the fact that users are 'prohibited to create, upload or share content that threatens the unity of India or public order, is pornographic, violates copyright or patent, or contains software virus'.[9] The then Union Minister of State for Electronics and Information Technology, Rajeev Chandrasekhar, announced publicly that the time for ambiguity on content that is harmful to citizens must end. Critics pointed out, however, that expecting the intermediary to decide on what constitutes prohibited content and make reasonable efforts to dissuade users from creating, uploading and sharing it raises the question of whether the intermediary is the right entity to make decisions that directly impact citizens' freedom of speech and expression.

The 2022 amendment also added a new layer to the existing architecture of the Grievance Appellate Committee, which would now adjudicate on appeals against the decisions of grievance officers. In April 2023 came further amendments, this time ostensibly to regulate online gaming. Its operative aspect however was to provide the Press Information Bureau, which is the propaganda wing of the government, with the power to fact-check any information related to the government, which intermediaries could be required to take down. If they do not do this upon being ordered to, their safe harbour status, which otherwise protects them from any liabilities caused by content generated by any user, could be in jeopardy.

These new stipulations were widely seen as undermining freedom of speech and expression in the country for several important reasons, the most important being that it allows the State to be chief arbiter on information concerning its own functioning, thereby making a mockery of Article 19(1)(a):

> The problem with government-mandated censorship arises primarily because the government holds a unique position of power, with access to an extensive range of communication channels that have the widest reach possible in society…. The government acts as both judge and the prosecutor when it comes to content related to its own business. (Singh 2023)

The IT Rules, introduced in 2021 as instrument to protect the citizen from harmful internet and social media content, evolved over the years to become a malleable tool to shore up the government's powers of censorship. When the two-part BBC documentary on Prime Minister Modi, 'The Modi Question', emerged in January 2023, it was immediately deemed by the government as 'hostile propaganda and anti-India garbage' (*BBC News* 2023). The Union Ministry of Information and Broadcasting lost no time in citing emergency powers under the IT Rules, 2021, to ensure that Twitter and YouTube disabled Indian citizens' access to the documentary. It is intriguing that in the emergency powers inherent in Rule 16(3) of the IT Rules as well as Section 69A of the IT Act, which allow the government to block out information, the term 'emergency' has not be defined. As Apar Gupta observed, the IT

Rules have become an 'everything law': 'Today it clothes violations of fundamental rights by creating the pretence of a procedure which permits unlimited censorship powers that are often left to an unbounded imagination and capriciousness' (*The Hindu* 2023).

An Avalanche of Laws to Control Digital Media

From 2022 onwards, the Ministry of Information and Broadcasting and the Ministry of Electronics and Information Technology got busy with a series of digital media laws and regulations even as the general election of 2024 drew closer.

In November 2022, the Ministry of Electronics and Information Technology released a draft of the Digital Personal Data Protection Bill. This happened to be the government's fourth attempt to come up with a data protection law in India, a journey which began in 2011 when the discussions were initiated by the Department of Personnel and Training on a privacy bill. It was meant to be the first legislative protection extended to personal data in post-independence India, and aimed to address general concerns about the State's overweening powers of surveillance over ordinary citizens through the use of the Indian Telegraph Act, 1885 and Section 69 of the Information Technology Act, 2000.

What sparked fears about the 2022 draft was that it provided blanket exemptions to certain government agencies. It led Justice B. N. Srikrishna, who had headed the drafting of an earlier version of the bill, to comment,

> The Data Board is a creation of the executive with no guidelines on its composition, establishment, qualifications of its chair and members, etc., and therefore it will be a captive of the government with little independence, if it is the regulator; if not, there is no regulator at all. (Saigal 2022)

His plea for a more robust regulatory regime was ignored. Other experts pointed out that a data protection board under this law could not possibly perform its function since it lacked autonomy and would be under the almost total control of the government. What was perhaps the most egregious aspect of this legislation, as noted by several analysts, was that it ignored the three tests that the Puttaswamy verdict had outlined: that the privacy right of the individual should be curtailed only for 'necessity', 'reasonably' and 'proportionately'.

Despite strident criticism of the legislation, the Government of India went on to pass it into law the following year. The blanket exemptions that had been critiqued at the drafting stage remained in the new law, which cited Article 19(2) to justify providing total immunity from its provisions to security agencies. It also had a severely limited mandate to address data breaches and allowed the government to go ahead and block access to websites that it deemed problematic. Of particular concern was the fact that the law seriously weakened the architecture of the Right to Information Act, 2005. Section 8(1) of the RTI Act already prevents anyone seeking personal information which has 'no relationship to any public activity or interest'. The new amendment to the Act did away with this clause, which meant that no 'personal information', regardless of whether it was of public interest or not, could now be accessed. Journalism was not exempted under the new law.

In 2022, the government also began work on a draft telecommunications bill to update the regulatory framework of the three foundational laws that controlled telecommunications in India, namely the Indian Telegraph Act, 1885, the Indian Wireless Telegraphy Act, 1933 and the Telegraph Wires (Unlawful) Possession Act, 1950. The most important feature of this proposed law was the expansion of what was understood as 'telecommunication services'. Over-the-top or OTT communication services—that is, content that is streamed through internet-connected devices—were now brought under its ambit. The licensing conditions hitherto applicable to telecom services providers were now extended to these services as well, allowing the government access to user data. The role of regulation, earlier invested with the Telecom Regulatory Authority of India, which had enjoyed a certain degree of independence, was handed over to the government. Also, for the first time, the government was empowered to order suspension of the internet without judicial oversight.

Internet analysts and activists warned that this draft exponentially increased the power of the government to control the telecommunications sector and weakened the independent regulatory structures that had governed it thus far. Even the definition of what constitutes 'telecommunications services' was made malleable and open to interpretation. It also seriously undermined privacy features in OTT services like end-to-end encryption. The manner in which it reinforced the government's power to suspend internet services without 'procedural safeguards envisaged in the SC's *Anuradha Bhasin* judgement such as the proportionality test, exploration of suitable alternatives and the adoption of least intrusive measures' (Kathuria and Suri 2024) was considered truly alarming. The draft legislation squandered 'the opportunity to restructure the telecom industry and adopt regulations that support user rights instead of infringing upon them' (Panwar and Singh 2024) and undermined rather than deepened the citizen's rights to freedom of speech and expression. It became the law of the land in December 2023.

One of the first moves made by the BJP-led government once it returned to power for a third term in June 2024, albeit as a coalition, was to bring into force certain provisions in the Telecommunications Act. This included Section 20(2), which empowered the government to stop the transmission of any information if it was deemed to threaten public safety. Central agencies like the Central Bureau of Investigation, the Enforcement Directorate and the Intelligence Bureau can now intercept telephonic communication with permission from the Union home ministry. This section also allows governments at the state and central levels to take temporary possession of any telecom service. The Telecom Cyber Security Rules introduced under this law in November 2024 bestowed the central government with the power to block, as it deems fit, the use of telecom equipment and allows it to access data from telecom entities.

Another draft legislation of 2023—the the Broadcasting Services (Regulation) Bill—sought to replace the Cable Television Networks (Regulation) Act which had regulated broadcasting in the country since 1995. It was very much in the mould of the laws just discussed and adopted the same feature that marked the IT Rules, 2021, in that a three-tiered system was proposed that was controlled ultimately by the Broadcast Advisory Council (BAC), comprising members whose appointments and tenures were dependent on the government. At the same time, broadcasters were required to set up their own structures for self-regulation and dispute redressal.

The draft broadcasting bill caused consternation among digital stakeholders for various reasons that had a direct bearing on the citizen's freedom of speech. *First*, it allowed the BAC to censor digital content in the 'public interest', which incidentally was not defined in the draft, enhancing the capacity for subjective interpretation on the part of the regulator. An internet rights organisation described it thus: 'Ambiguous definitions, uncertainty over scope of application, and reliance on future rulemaking by the executive makes the Broadcasting Bill vague, overbroad, and worrisome, that is open for misuse through subjective and selective application' (Internet Freedom Foundation 2023).

Second, the government was empowered under the bill not just to inspect broadcasters without intimation, but to impound their equipment if necessary.

Third, it sought to bring the entire broadcasting industry under a single legislative umbrella. While streaming services and news and current affairs in the digital space have not been subject to government regulation thus far, under this bill they were required to mandatorily register themselves with the government. This included individuals who conducted podcasts or ran news programmes on YouTube. The government thus acquired the power, through this bill, to deny these entities registration, or withdraw their registration at any point, creating conditions for pre-censorship with news 'being put into a Central Board of Film Certification or CBFC inspired regime reserved for cinema' (Chisti 2023). The potentially chilling effect of this bill, should it come into force, will be felt not just in the online space but in the news space more generally.

The blowback to the draft broadcasting bill from civil society and media activists has restrained the government's hand. The draft of the bill that had been circulated earlier was withdrawn and the government promised further consultations on it.

The year 2023 was certainly an extraordinary year of lawmaking that sought to strip citizens of many of their media rights. It saw, for instance, the Post Office Act, 2023, replacing its British Raj counterpart. The new postal law considerably enhanced the government's powers of intercepting posted material without laying down the necessary guard rails, like a grievance redressal mechanism for those whose privacy rights were unlawfully violated (Khan 2023).

The Press and Registration of Periodicals Act, 2023, repealing the colonial-era Press and Registration of Books Act, 1867, came into force in early 2024. Although it was hailed by the government as 'yet another step of the Modi Government towards jettisoning mentality of slavery and bringing new laws for new India' (*The Indian Express* 2023), it was seen as bringing yet another layer of governmental control over digital media.

More laws, especially those dealing with the digital space, are on the anvil. For instance, in March 2023, the Ministry of Electronics and Information Technology made a presentation on its proposed omnibus law, the Digital India Bill that is to replace the Information Technology Act of 2000. Once again, going by the initial signals from the ministry, the emphasis will be on regulation and the 'urgent need for a specialised and dedicated adjudicatory mechanism for online civil and criminal offences' (Press Information Bureau 2023). It may see the discarding of the 'safe harbour' provisions for online platforms and heavy punishment for any violations of the law. The general election to the 18th Lok Sabha delayed its enactment.

Digital giants, prompted not so much by the pressure to ensure free speech for their users as by their own business interests, are pushing back on the government's attempts to control their operations. WhatsApp and Facebook/Meta are challenging Rule 4(2) of the IT Rules, 2021, in Indian courts, with WhatsApp maintaining that the obligation to provide information of the originator of the message would break its end-to-end encryption of user messages. In a firm statement made in court, WhatsApp asserted, 'As a platform, we are saying that if we are told to break encryption, then WhatsApp will cease its operations' (*The Hindu* 2024). X (earlier Twitter) has taken the Union government to court for issuing takedown orders through its Sahyog Portal, which it argues amounts to censorship without due process. The Karnataka High Court is hearing the case.

Online news and opinion portals also set up their own bodies in order to both respond to governmental strictures and actions as well as for self-regulation. In 2020, 11 digital-only organisations came together to institute an organisation, DIGIPUB News India Foundation, that would 'represent, amplify and evolve best practices to build a robust digital news ecology that is truly world-class, independent and upholds the highest standards of journalism' in India. Given that Section 12 of the IT Rules, 2021, mandated such self-regulatory bodies, other bodies sprang up too, including the Professional News Broadcasting Standards Authority (NBF), the Confederation of Online Media (India) and the Web Journalists' Standards Authority.

Some of these bodies, along with individual digital news portals, challenged the IT Rules in courts across the country and occasionally received favourable verdicts. For instance, the Bombay High Court in its August 2021 ruling stayed Rules 9(1) and 9(3) of the IT Rules, which mandatorily imposed adherence to the Code of Ethics, saying that this could amount to violating the freedom of speech guarantee. An estimated 12 petitions challenging the rules which piled up in the Supreme Court have now been transferred to the Delhi High Court for a comprehensive verdict.

The government, however, has not ceased its attempts to tighten control. In 2023, it tweaked Rule 3(1)(b)(v) of the IT Rules to allow the setting up of a fact check unit (FCU) to look into digital coverage of matters involving the GOI. The FCU was to be administered by the government controlled Press Information Bureau, which meant that the government could now sit in judgement on any digital media content relating to it. The Bombay High Court struck down the FCU in September 2024, ruling that 'under the right to freedom of speech and expression, there is no further "right to truth", nor is it the responsibility of the state to ensure that the citizens are entitled only to "information" that was not fake or misleading as identified by the FCU' (Philipose 2024).

Are We Witnessing Digital Authoritarianism?

The question raised by observers of a digital media sector that is now being subjected to several legislative controls is an important one: are we witnessing the rise of digital authoritarianism?

Internet users in the country rose from 5.5 million in the year 2005[10] to over 880 million by March 2023 (*The Hindu Businessline* 2023). Crimes that could never be imagined even a decade ago, like deepfakes and revenge porn, have now become commonplace. Given the time lag that inevitably occurs between changes in the law and the innovations in digital media technologies as well as shifts in digital practices, the government is necessarily required to display an alertness of response to the negative impacts they could have on the lives of its citizens. The worry is that a government looking to clamp down on freedoms could seize upon external circumstances to tighten its control.

Three developments in the first half of 2025 seem to point in this direction. The outcry over inappropriate comments made by YouTuber Ranveer Allahbadia in February 2025 led the government to alert the Standing Committee on Communications and Information Technology about a 'growing demand for a stricter and effective legal framework to regulate harmful content'. Similarly, the terrorist attack at Pahalgam of 22 April 2025, which claimed the lives of at least 26 Indian tourists, immediately prompted actions like the banning of YouTube channels and the filing of police cases against Indian satirists on YouTube whose content was seen as undermining the government's stances (*Scroll.in* 2025). This was followed by the arrest on 18 May 2025 of Ashoka University professor Ali Khan Mahmudabad, over some benign comments he made on Facebook on how the projection of a Muslim spokeswomen during Operation Sindoor was welcome but could be deemed hypocritical if there was no change in the way minorities in the country were being treated (Yadav 2025).

The manner in which these actions were taken indicates that they are inevitably overbroad in their interpretations of the law and marked by a repressive footprint. The intention seems to be to control and tailor public conversations to conform to the State's own narrative. It is this that has fuelled the view that India is today witnessing the rise of digital authoritarianism. For any Indian who values the great efforts made by members of the Constituent Assembly to enshrine the words 'All citizens shall have the right to freedom of speech and expression' in the Indian Constitution, this cannot but be a source of great concern. The Supreme Court, as protector of the Constitution, has spoken out against this trend, stating that 'the ability to freely express one's thoughts and views is a fundamental aspect of human dignity' (Bedi 2025).

Notes

1. Speech delivered at the India Telecom Conference 2007. Available at https://archivepmo.nic.in/drmanmohansingh/speech-details.php?nodeid=607 (accessed February 2025).

2. Writ Petition (Civil) No. 1031 of 2019. Available at https://main.sci.gov.in/supremecourt/2019/28817/28817_2019_2_1501_19350_Judgement_10-Jan-2020.pdf (accessed February 2025).

3. *Shreya Singhal v. U.O.I* on 24 March 2015. Available at https://indiankanoon.org/doc/110813550/ (accessed February 2025).

4. *Shreya Singhal v. U.O.I.*

5. *Shreya Singhal v. U.O.I.*

6. See https://digitalindia.gov.in/ (accessed Februaru 2025).

7. See 'Social Media in India - 2023 Stats & Platform Trends', available at https://oosga.com/social-media/ind/ (accessed February 2025).

8. 'Justice K.S.Puttaswamy(Retd) vs Union Of India', 2018, retrieved from https://indiankanoon.org/doc/127517806/.

9. See https://prsindia.org/billtrack/amendments-to-it-rules-2021 (accessed February 2025).

10. See https://www.researchgate.net/figure/1-Number-of-Internet-Users-in-India-2000-to-2016_tbl1_328566697 (accessed February 2025).

Afterword

If democracy in India is to survive, it will need the constitutional ballast provided by Article 19(1)(a). The Supreme Court of India has recognised in innumerable verdicts, right from the days of *Romesh Thapar v. State of Madras*, 1950, that the right to freedom of speech necessarily implies a free press/media; which also means that if freedom of the media is to survive, it will need the legislative buttress of Article 19(1)(a). Major verdicts over the decades expanded on the import of the Article in terms of everyday life. *Justice K. S. Puttaswamy (retd) v. Union of India*, 2018, recognised its centrality in the expression of one's sexual orientation and religious beliefs, which in turn has a close relationship with freedom of speech. More recently, in its February 2024 ruling on the electoral bonds case, the Supreme Court emphatically reiterated the importance of this Article. One of the reasons the electoral bonds scheme needed to be immediately discontinued, it had argued, was that it violated the voters' right to information inherent in Article 19(1)(a).

Over the years, as we have seen in these pages, serious attempts have been made by both State and private actors to undermine media freedoms in variegated ways and from all indications these attempts to skew the Indian public sphere in order to control opinion and the national narrative will continue to be a major challenge in the future.

Afterword

The raid by the Delhi Police on the portal *NewsClick* and the arrest of its founding editor in October 2023 is just one instance of the State's overweening drive to repress those media organisations that have chosen to chart an independent course (*NewsClick* 2023). The raids were conducted on media persons associated with *NewsClick* in 88 locations, in Delhi and elsewhere in the country, without any formal warrants. Journalists' devices, like mobile phones and laptops, were peremptorily confiscated without receipts or hash values being issued. Some of the best known journalists in the country were thus robbed almost instantly of their capacity to think, question, reason, document, report, write or speak.

The modus operandi of media control by private actors takes other routes but can be equally destructive of the right to a free media. Through the last decade we have seen the takeover of significant sections of the media by large corporate houses, using their financial, social and political capital. In 2014, Reliance Industries Limited, owned by Mukesh Ambani, acquired Network18 Media & Investments Ltd, as well as its subsidiary, TV18 Broadcast Ltd, and thus came to control a large swathe of the national media. In December 2022, one of India's richest men, Gautam Adani, acquired a majority stake in New Delhi Television Ltd (NDTV), a relatively independent news channel. The impact on the independence of the reportage of these organisations was immediate.

Revisiting Article 19(1)(a), which has sometimes been described as the heart and soul of the Indian Constitution, as this book attempts to do, is also to remind ourselves of the need to protect and defend it.

References

Abdullah, Hasan. 2006. 'Urdu in India'. In *Redefining Urdu Politics in India*, edited by Ather Farouqui. New Delhi: Oxford University Press.

Acker, Yolanda F. 2022. 'Radio Music in Civil-war Madrid'. *The Volunteer*. Available at https://albavolunteer.org/2022/05/music-on-the-radio-in-madrid-during-the-spanish-civil-war/ (accessed February 2025).

Agarwal, Surabhi and Geetika Rustagi. 2012. 'Arrest for tweets against FM's son raises new fears'. *Mint*, 2 November. Available at https://www.livemint.com/Politics/nSMOJy0NzUiK6N0e5M0f0N/Arrest-for-tweets-against-FMs-son-raises-new-fears.html (accessed February 2025).

Agrawal, Ravi. 2018. *India Connected: How the Smartphone is Transforming the World's Largest Democracy*. New Delhi: Oxford University Press.

Ananth, V. Krishna. 2020a. *Between Freedom and Unfreedom: The Press in Independent India*. New Delhi: The Alcove.

———. 2020b. 'India's Free Press Is Still Tormented by the Laws Brought by the Emergency'. *The Wire*, 25 June. Available at https://thewire.in/history/emergency-free-press (accessed February 2025).

Anderson, Benedict. 1991. *Imagined Communities: Reflections on the Origin and Spread of Nationalism*, second edition. London: Verso Books.

Annual Status of Education Report (ASER). 2017. *Annual Status of Education Report (Rural)*. Available at https://asercentre.org/aser-2017/ (accessed February 2025).

Arshi, Arshdeep. 2019. 'Jallianwala Centenary: The British journalist who exposed "Dyerarchy" in Amritsar'. *Hindustan Times*, 7 April. Available at https://www.hindustantimes.com/chandigarh/jallianwala-centenary-the-british-journalist-who-exposed-dyerarchy-in-amritsar/story-JFcg3gJKDLXB6VyEZVameN.html (accessed February 2025).

References

Athique, Adrian. 2012. *Indian Media: Global Approaches*. Cambridge: Polity Press.

Austin, Granville. 1966. *The Indian Constitution: Cornerstone of a Nation*. Oxford: Clarendon Press.

Balaji, J. 2010. 'PCI sidelines sub-committee report on "paid news"'. *The Hindu*, 30 July. Available at https://www.thehindu.com/news/national/PCI-sidelines-sub-committee-report-on-ldquopaid-newsrdquo/article16215657.ece (accessed February 2025).

Balkin, Jack M. 2004. 'Digital Speech and Democratic Culture: A Theory of Freedom of Expression for the Information Society'. *New York University Law Review* 79(1): 1–58.

Bayly, C. A. 1999. *Empire and Information: Intelligence Gathering and Social Communication in India, 1780–1870*. Cambridge: Cambridge University Press.

BBC News. 2020. 'The fiery Indian student who ran a secret radio station for independence', 14 August. Available at https://www.bbc.com/news/world-asia-india-53775313 (accessed February 2025).

———. 2023. 'BBC ordered to Delhi High Court over Modi documentary', 22 May. Available at https://www.bbc.com/news/world-asia-india-65670818 (accessed February 2025).

Beijing Platform for Action. 1995. 'Chapter IV. J. Women and Media'. Available at http://un-documents.net/bpa-4-j.htm (accessed February 2025).

Bhagat, R. B., et al. 2018. *Access to Household Amenities and Assets in India: An Analysis of Census Data*. Research monograph, International Institute for Population Sciences, Mumbai.

Bharthur, Parthasarathy Sanjay. 1989. 'The Role of Insitutional Relationships in Communication Technology Transfer: A Case Study of the Indian National Satellite System'. PhD thesis submitted to Simon Fraser University, Canada.

Bhatia, Gautam. 2016. *Offend, Shock, Or Disturb: Free Speech under the Indian Constitution*. New Delhi: Oxford University Press.

———. 2019. *The Transformative Constitution: A Radical Biography in Nine Acts*. New Delhi: HarperCollins India.

———. 2023. 'Top court must strike down the sedition law'. *Hindustan Times*, 6 June.

Bhushan, Sandeep. 2019. *The Indian Newsroom Studios: Stars and the Unmaking of Reporters*. Chennai: Westland Books.

Bombay Union of Journalists. 1988. 'Scrap Defamation Bill!' Available at https://mediavigil.com/wp-content/uploads/2018/01/15.-Bombay-Union-of-Journalists-Scrap-Defamation-Bill-Bombay....pdf (accessed February 2025).

Borders, William. 1975. 'India Arrests One of Her Most Important Journalists'. *The New York Times*, 26 July.

Brass, Paul. 2000. 'The Strong State and the Fear of Disorder'. In *Transforming India: Social and Political Dynamics of Democracy*, edited by Francine Frankel, Zoya Hasan, Rajeev Bhargava and Balveer Arora. New Delhi: Oxford University Press.

Burra, Arudra V. 2019: 'Civil liberties in the early constitution: The *CrossRoads* and *Organiser* cases'. In *Human Rights in India*, edited by Satvinder Juss. London: Routledge.

Business Standard. 2015. 'PM Modi's "Mann ki Baat" is misuse of government machinery, says Congress', 15 September. Available at https://www.business-standard.com/article/news-ani/pm-modi-s-mann-ki-baat-is-misuse-of-government-machinery-says-congress-115091600477_1.html (accessed February 2025).

Castells, Manuel. 2013. *Communication Power*. Oxford: Oxford University Press.

Chatterji, P. C. 1987. *Broadcasting in India*. New Delhi: Sage Publications.

Chaturvedi, J. P. 1992. 'Introduction'. *The Indian Press at Crossroads*. New Delhi: Media Research Associates.

Chishti, Seema. 2023. 'Control + All or Delete: The Draft Broadcast Bill Is a Blueprint for Censorship'. *The Wire.in*, 7 December. Available at https://thewire.in/government/control-all-or-delete-the-draft-broadcast-bill-is-a-blueprint-for-censorship (accessed February 2025).

Constituent Assembly Debates. 1946. *Constituent Assembly Debates on 13 December, 1946*. Available at https://indiankanoon.org/doc/548244/ (accessed February 2025).

———. 1948a. *Constituent Assembly Debates on 1 December, 1948*. Available at https://indiankanoon.org/doc/1107530/ (accessed February 2025).

Constituent Assembly Debates. 1948b. *Constituent Assembly Debates on 2 December, 1948*. Available at https://indiankanoon.org/doc/1389880/ (accessed February 2025).

Desai, Ketaki. 2023. 'Deepfakes are eroding trust. How do we even know if a real video is real?' Interview with Hany Farid. *The Times of India*, 19 November.

Draboo, Shailla. 2020. 'Financial Inclusion and Digital India: A Critical Assessment'. *Economic and Political Weekly* 55(17). Available at https://www.epw.in/engage/article/financial-inclusion-and-digital-india-critical (accessed February 2025).

Dutta, Amrita Nayak. 2018. 'Modi govt may turn DD and AIR into public sector firms, disband Prasar Bharati'. *The Print*, 24 July. Available at https://theprint.in/india/governance/modi-govt-may-turn-dd-and-air-into-public-sector-firms-disband-prasar-bharati/87678/ (accessed February 2025).

Economic and Political Weekly. 1988. 'Defamation Bill: High Political Status'. 23(37): 1868.

Editors' Guild of India. 2002. *Rights and Wrongs: Ordeal by Fire in the Killing Fields of Gujarat*. Fact Finding Mission Report, 3 May.

———. 2023. *Report of the Fact-Finding Mission on Media's Reportage of the Ethnic Violence in Manipur*, 2 September. Available at https://editorsguild.in/wp-content/uploads/2023/09/EGI-report-on-Manipur.pdf (accessed February 2025).

Emmanuel, Meera. 2018. '"If hereafter things go wrong, we will have nobody to blame", Dr. Ambedkar's final speech in Constituent Assembly'. *Bar and Bench*, 14 April. Available at https://www.barandbench.com/columns/dr-ambedkar-1949-constituent-assembly-speech (accessed February 2025).

Fernandes, Leela. 2006. *India's New Middle Class: Democratic Politics in an Era of Economic Reform*. New Delhi: Oxford University Press.

Gandhi, Shailesh. 2025. 'The RTI is now the "right to deny information"'. *The Hindu*, 25 February. Available at https://www.thehindu.com/opinion/lead/the-rti-is-now-the-right-to-deny-information/article69259261.ece (accessed February 2025).

Gaur, Ratika. 2023. 'Public Order (v Sedition) vs Freedom of Speech and Expression: A Legal Discourse on the Limits of Indian Rationality in the Public Sphere'. *Economic and Political Weekly* 58(11). Available at https://www.epw.in/journal/2023/11/perspectives/public-order-v-sedition-vs-freedom-speech-and.html (accessed February 2025).

Ghosh, Shauvik and Ashish K. Mishra. 2015. 'The birth of the Internet in India'. *Mint*, 30 June. Available at https://www.livemint.com/Industry/R3kgewhIhKscbiELV1sHZM/The-birth-of-the-Internet-in-India.html (accessed February 2025).

Government of India. 1951. *The Parliamentary Debates: Third Session of the Parliament of India*, 29 May. Available at https://eparlib.nic.in/bitstream/123456789/760712/1/ppd_29-05-1951.pdf (accessed February 2025).

———. 1961. 3rd Five Year Plan (1961–1966). New Delhi: Planning Commission of India.

———. 1977. *White Paper on Misuse of Mass Media during the Internal Emergency*, August. New Delhi. Available at https://ebin.pub/white-paper-on-misuse-of-mass-media-during-the-internal-emergency-august-1977.html (accessed February 2025).

———. 1997. 9th Five Year Plan (1997–2002), volume 2. New Delhi: Planning Commission. Available at https://web.archive.org/web/20150121020841/http://planningcommission.gov.in/plans/planrel/fiveyr/index9.html (accessed February 2025).

Guha, Ramachandra. 2020. 'What Modi Could Learn From Lal Bahadur Shastri—Ramachandra Guha'. *NDTV* Opinion, 2 October. Available at https://www.ndtv.com/opinion/what-modi-could-learn-from-lal-bahadur-shastri-ramachandra-guha-2303731 (accessed February 2025).

Gupta, Apar. 2010. 'Balancing Online Privacy in India'. *Indian Journal of Law and Technology* 6(1): 43–64.

———. 2023. 'India's juggernaut of censorship'. *The Hindu*, 26 January.

Halder, Debarati and H. Jaishankar. 2017. *Cyber Crimes against Women in India*. New Delhi: Sage.

Hindustan Times. 2015. 'New panel to work on Section 66A alternative', 14 April. Available at https://www.hindustantimes.com/india/new-panel-to-work-on-section-66a-alternative/story-WOBxNKeUQsVfeifkozE3tL.html (accessed February 2025).

———. 2022 [1951]. 'Clause on Freedom of Speech Amended', *HT* This Day: 26 May, 1951.

Human Rights Watch. 2023. 'India: Arrests, Raids Target Critics of Government', 13 October. Available at https://www.hrw.org/news/2023/10/13/india-arrests-raids-target-critics-government (accessed February 2025).

India Today. 1990. 'Killing of AIR official in Chandigarh shows newsmen too are targeted by militants in Punjab', 30 December. Available at https://www.indiatoday.in/magazine/special-report/story/19901231-killing-of-air-official-in-chandigarh-shows-newsmen-too-are-targeted-by-militants-in-punjab-813465-1990-12-30 (accessed February 2025).

———. 1994. 'We found that regional languages were not getting enough time: K.P. Singh Deo', 31 January.

International Monitor Institute Records. 1993–2001 and undated. 'Rwanda Archive Subseries'. David M. Rubenstein Rare Book & Manuscript Library. Durham: Duke University.

Internet Freedom Foundation. 2023. 'Dear MIB, kill the bill and #LetUsChill'. Available at https://internetfreedom.in/comments-on-the-broadcasting-bill-2023/ (accessed February 2025).

Jaiman, Ashish. 2023. 'The danger of deepfakes'. *The Hindu*, 1 January.

Jeffrey, Robin. 1994. 'Monitoring Newspapers and Understanding the Indian State'. *Asia Survey* 34(8): 748–763. Available at https://doi.org/10.2307/2645262 (accessed February 2025).

———. 2000. *India's Newspaper Revolution Capitalism, Politics and the Indian-language Press, 1977–99*. New Delhi: Oxford University Press.

———. 2001. '[NOT] being there: Dalits and India's newspapers'. *South Asia: Journal of South Asian Studies* 24(2): 225–238.

Jeffrey, Robin and Assa Doron. 2013. *Cell Phone Nation*. New Delhi: Hachette.

Kagal, Ayesha, ed. 2016. *More News is Good News: 25 Years of NDTV*. New Delhi: HarperCollins India.

Kapoor, Coomi. 2015. *The Emergency: A Personal History*. New Delhi: Penguin/Viking.

Kathuria, Rajat and Isha Suri. 2024. 'How the Telecom Act undermines personal liberties'. *The Indian Express*, 25 January. Available at https://indianexpress.com/article/opinion/columns/how-the-telecom-act-undermines-personal-liberties-9126314/ (accessed February 2025).

Kaul, Chandrika. 2003. *Reporting the Raj: The British Press and India, c. 1880–1992*. New York: Manchester University Press.

Khan, Khadija. 2023. 'Post Office Bill, 2023: Why it was brought in, provisions, criticism'. *The Indian Express*, 16 December. Available at https://indianexpress.com/article/explained/explained-law/post-office-bill-shashi-tharoor-9070808/ (accessed February 2025).

Khanna, Sundeep. 2021. 'Backstory: When Siva stormed the Indian PC market'. *CNBC TV18*, 9 March.

Khosla, Madhav. 2012. *The Indian Constitution*, Oxford India Short Introductions. New Delhi: Oxford University Press.

Kohli-Khandekar, Vanita. 2013. *The Indian Media Business*, fourth edition. New Delhi: Sage.

Kothari, Rajni. 1961. 'Form and Substance in Indian Politics'. *Economic and Political Weekly* 13(21): 819–826.

Kripalani, Coonoor. 2017. 'Building Nationhood through Broadcast Media in Postcolonial India'. *Contemporary Postcolonial Asia, Association for Asian Studies* 22(1). Available at https://www.asianstudies.org/publications/eaa/archives/building-nationhood-through-broadcast-media-in-postcolonial-india/ (accessed February 2025).

Krishnan, Vidya. 2023. 'A Billionaire, a TV Network, and the Fight for a Free Press in India'. *Nieman Reports*, 24 July. Available at https://niemanreports.org/articles/india-ndtv-modi/ (accessed February 2025).

Kruthika, R. 2020. 'Freedom of the Press: A Constitutional History'. Bengaluru: Centre for Law and Policy Research.

Kumar, Sashi. 2013. 'Lend me your ears'. *Frontline*, 1 April. Available at https://frontline.thehindu.com/columns/Sashi_Kumar/lend-me-your-ears/article4569545.ece (accessed February 2025).

Kumar, Shanti. 2014. 'Spaces of Television Rethinking the Public/Private Divide in Postcolonial India'. In *Channeling Cultures: Television Studies from India*, edited by Biswarup Sen and Abhijit Roy. New Delhi: Oxford University Press.

Kumar, Smarika. 2016. 'Concentration of Media Ownership and the Imagination of Free Speech'. *Economic and Political Weekly* 51(17): 127–133.

Laghate, Gaurav. 2022. 'Adani Group acquires NDTV promoters' additional 27.26% stake for Rs 602 crore'. *Mint*, 30 December. Available at https://www.livemint.com/companies/news/adani-group-acquires-ndtv-promoters-additional-27-26-stake-for-rs-602-cr-11672388372078.html (accessed February 2025).

Liang, Lawrence. 2016. 'Free Speech and Expression'. In *The Oxford Handbook of the Indian Constitution*, edited by Sujit Choudhry, Madhav Khosla and Pratap Bhanu Mehta. New Delhi: Oxford University Press.

LiveLaw.in. 2021. 'India's New IT Rules Do Not Conform With International Human Rights Norms: UN Special Rapporteurs', 19 June. Available at https://www.livelaw.in/news-updates/indias-new-it-rules-do-not-conform-with-international-human-rights-norms-un-special-rapporteurs-175978 (accessed Febaruary 2025).

Mahapatra, Dhananjay. 2021. '"Terrible, shocking" that Sec 66A still used to arrest people: Supreme Court'. *The Times of India*, 6 July. Available at https://timesofindia.indiatimes.com/india/terrible-shocking-that-sec-66a-still-used-to-arrest-people-supreme-court/articleshow/84159436.cms (accessed February 2025).

Majumder, Kunal. 2023. 'Lawyer Apar Gupta on what the Indian Supreme Court's order on COVID-19 coverage means for journalists'. In *Media, Migrants, And the Pandemic in India: A Reader*, edited by Bharat Bhushan. New Delhi: Routledge.

Mankekar, D. R. 1984. 'Free Not Independent'. In *What Ails the Indian Press*, edited by R. C. S. Sarkar. New Delhi: S. Chand & Company Ltd.

Mankekar, Purnima. 2014. 'Televisusal Temporalities and the Affective Organization of Everyday Life'. In *Channeling Cultures: Television Studies from India*, edited by Biswarup Sen and Abhijit Roy. New Delhi: Oxford University Press.

McChesney, Robert W. 2013. *Digital Disconnect: How Capitalism is Turning the Internet Against Democracy*. New York: New Press.

McDermott, Rachell Fell, Leonard A. Gordon, et al., eds. 2015. *Sources of Indian Traditions: Modern India, Pakistan and Bangladesh*. New York: Columbia University Press.

MediaClassification.org. n. d. 'Chanda Committee Report'. Available at https://mediaclassification.org/timeline-event/chanda-committee-report-india/ (accessed February 2025).

Mehta, Nalin. 2014. 'When Live News Was Too Dangerous'. In *Channeling Cultures: Television Studies from India*, edited by Biswarup Sen and Abhijit Roy. New Delhi: Oxford University Press.

———. 2015. *Behind a Billion Screens*. New Delhi: HarperCollins India.

Mirchandani, G. G., ed. 1976. *Indian Backgrounders—Television in India*. Vikrant Press.

Mondal, Sudipto. 2017. 'Indian media wants Dalit news but not Dalit reporters'. *Al Jazeera*, 2 June. Available at https://www.aljazeera.com/opinions/2017/6/2/indian-media-wants-dalit-news-but-not-dalit-reporters (accessed February 2025).

Muralidharan, Sukumar. 2007. 'Broadcast Regulation and Public Right to Know'. *Economic and Political Weekly* 42(9): 743–751.

———. 2018. *Freedom, Civility, Commerce: Contemporary Media and the Public*. New Delhi: Three Essays Collective.

Nair, Tara S. 2003. 'Growth and Structural Transformation of Newspaper Industry in India'. *Economic and Political Weekly* 38(39): 4182–4189.

Narayan, Sunetra Sen. 2014. *Globalization and Television: A Study of the Indian Experience 1990–2020*. New Delhi: Oxford University Press.

Narayan, Sunetra Sen and Shalini Narayanan. 2016. 'An Overview of New Media in India'. In *India Connected: Mapping the Impact of New Media*. New Delhi: Sage.

Ninan, T. N. 1984. 'New policy allows computer companies to produce as much as they can'. *India Today*, 15 December.

NewsClick. 2023. 'One Month after NewsClick Raids, Journalists Express Concern over Declining Press Freedom', 3 November. Available at https://www.newsclick.in/one-month-after-newsclick-raids-journalists-express-concern-over-declining-press-freedom (accessed February 2025).

Pal, Joyojeet and Syeda Zainab Akbar. 2020. 'It's Essential to Sift Through Hate-Driven Misinformation on Coronavirus'. *The Wire*, 25 March. Available at https://thewire.in/media/coronavirus-misinformation-hate-fake-news (accessed February 2025).

Pande, Mrinal. 2022. *The Journey of Hindi Language Journalism in India*. New Delhi: Orient BlackSwan.

Panwar, Aryan and Varun Pratap Singh. 2024. 'Analysing the Telecommunications Act 2023: Is it a Draconian Law?' *Livelaw. in*, 4 June. Available at https://www.livelaw.in/lawschool/articles/analysing-the-telecommunications-act-2023-is-it-a-draconian-law-259612 (accessed February 2025).

Philipose, Pamela. 2019. *Media's Shifting Terrain: Five Years that Transformed the Way India Communicates*. New Delhi: Orient BlackSwan.

―――. 2021. 'Backstory: From "Partly Unfree" to "Fully Unfree"? The New IT Rules Could Hasten the Slide'. *The Wire*, 13 March. Available at https://thewire.in/media/backstory-india-democracy-new-it-rules (accessed February 2025).

―――. 2024. 'Backstory: The Government's Fact Check Unit is on Ice. But For How Long?'. *The Wire*, 28 September. Retrieved from https://thewire.in/government/backstory-the-governments-fact-check-unit-is-on-ice-but-for-how-long (accessed February 2025).

Pinney, Christopher. 2012. 'Iatrogenic Religion and Politics'. In *Censorship in South Asia: Cultural Regulation from Sedition to Seduction*, edited by Raminder Kaur and William Mazzarella. Routledge.

Prasad, Nandini. 1996. 'Media Policy and Women's Issues'. In *National Media Policy*, edited by V. S. Gupta and Rajeshwar Dyal. New Delhi: Concept Publishing Company.

Prasar Bharati. n. d. Chapter 1. In *AIR Manual*. New Delhi: Government of India. Available at https://prasarbharati.gov.in/wp-content/uploads/2024/04/Chapter1.pdf (accessed February 2025).

―――. 2020. *Annual Report, 2019–2020*. Available at https://prasarbharati.gov.in/wp-content/uploads/annual_report/AnnualReport-English-2019-20.pdf (accessed February 2025).

Press Information Bureau. 2023. 'MoS Rajeev Chandrasekhar holds consultations with stakeholders on the proposed Digital India Bill (DIB)', March. Available at https://www.pib.gov.in/PressReleasePage.aspx?PRID=1905639 (accessed February 2025).

Purkayastha, Prabir. 1985. 'Computer Policy & a Policy of Computerisation'. *Social Scientist* 13(7/8): 72–81.

Rajagopal, Krishnadas. 2018. 'What is the Prasar Bharati Act all about?' *The Hindu*, 10 March. Available at https://www.thehindu.com/news/national/what-is-the-prasar-bharati-act-all-about/article61869592.ece (accessed February 2025).

Rajaraman, V. 2015. 'History of Computing In India (1955–2010)'. *IEEE Annals of the History of Computing* 37(1): 24–35.

Raman, P. 2018. *The Post-Truth Media's Survival Sutra: A Footsoldier's Version*. New Delhi: Aakar Books.

Rao, P. S. V. 2008. 'TIFRAC, India's First Computer—A Retrospective'. *Resonance*, May: 420–429. Available at https://www.ias.ac.in/article/fulltext/reso/013/05/0420-0429 (accessed February 2025).

Report of the Expert Committee on Prasar Bharati. 2014. New Delhi: Government of India.

Report of the Press Commission, Part 1. 1954. New Delhi: Manager of Publications, Government of India.

Report of the Radio Broadcast Policy Committee. 2003. New Delhi: Manager of Publications, Government of India.

Report of the Second Press Commission, volume 1. 1982. New Delhi: Manager of Publications, Government of India.

Report of the Working Journalists Wage Committee. 1959. New Delhi: Manager of Publications, Government of India.

Saigal, Sonam. 2022. 'New draft of Data Protection Bill is fundamentally flawed, says Justice B.N. Srikrishna'. *The Hindu*, 25 November. Available at https://www.thehindu.com/opinion/interview/new-draft-of-data-protection-bill-is-fundamentally-flawed-says-justice-b-n-srikrishna/article66184338.ece (accessed February 2025).

Saksena, Nivedita and Siddhartha Srivastava. 2014. 'An Analysis of the Modern Offence of Sedition'. *NUJS Law Review* 7(2): 121–147.

Salunke, Pratik. 2015. 'Section 66A scrapped: Two years later, Palghar women finally get justice'. *Mint*, 24 March. Available at https://www.hindustantimes.com/mumbai/section-66a-scrapped-two-years-later-palghar-women-finally-get-justice/story-chZhP1jZHZ1NrES3026921.html (accessed February 2025).

Sarabhai, Vikram, et al. 1970. 'Insat—A National Satellite For Television And Telecommunication'. Paper presented at the National Conference on Electronics, Bombay.

Sayani, Ameen. 2020. 'The strange and amusing history of Indian Commercial Radio—Ameen Sayani'. *History for Peace*. Available at https://www.historyforpeace.pw/post/the-strange-and-amusing-history-of-indian-commercial-radio (accessed February 2025).

Scroll.in. 2023. 'Prasar Bharati signs news feed deal with RSS-backed agency', 27 February. Available at https://scroll.in/latest/1044672/prasar-bharati-signs-news-feed-deal-with-rss-backed-agency (accessed February 2025).

———. 2025. 'UP: Satirist, singer booked for "objectionable" posts about Pahalgam terror attack', 29 April. Available at https://scroll.in/latest/1081787/up-satirist-singer-booked-for-objectionable-posts-about-pahalgam-terror-attack (accessed May 2025).

Sen, Biswarup and Abhijit Roy, eds. 2014. *Channeling Cultures: Television Studies from India*. New Delhi: Oxford University Press.

Sen, Ronojoy. 2021. 'Charisma through Communication: Comparing Modi's Media Strategy to Nehru and Indira'. *Economic and Political Weekly* 56(10). Available at https://www.epw.in/engage/article/charisma-through-communication-comparing-modis (accessed February 2025).

Sengupta, A. 1996. 'Satellite Communication—Empowerment At Panchayat Level'. In *National Media Policy*, edited by Rajeshwar Dyal and V. S. Gupta. New Delhi: Concept Publishing.

Sethi, Devika. 2019. *War over Words: Censorship in India, 1930–1960*. Cambridge: Cambridge University Press

Shah, Amrita. 2019. *Telly-Gullotined: How Television Changed India*. New Delhi: Yoda Press and Sage Books.

Shrivastava, K. M. 1989. *Radio and TV Journalism*. New Delhi: Sterling Publishers.

Singh, Aadvik. 2024. 'DD News prime time: Funded by the public, against the public'. *Newslaundry.com*, 1 November. Available at https://www.newslaundry.com/2024/11/01/dd-news-primetime-funded-by-the-public-against-the-public (accessed February 2025).

Singh, Hemendra. 2023. 'The IT Amendment Rules, 2023: Censorship in the Guise of Fact-checking'. *Economic and Political Weekly* 58(43). Available at https://www.epw.in/journal/2023/43/commentary/it-amendment-rules-2023.html (accessed February 2025).

Singh, Nihal. 1992. *Your Slip Is Showing: Indian Press Today*. New Delhi: UBS Publishers.

Sinha, Bhadra. 2016. 'TN govt filed over 200 defamation cases for "derogatory remarks" against CM Jaya'. *Hindustan Times*, 22 August. Available at https://www.hindustantimes.com/india-news/tn-govt-filed-over-200-defamation-cases-for-derogatory-remarks-against-cm-jaya/story-b2vgfBs3Hwo98QRSrqdwYO.html (accessed February 2025).

Sorabjee, Soli J. 1977. *The Emergency, Censorship and the Press in India, 1975–77*. London: Writers and Scholars Educational Trust.

South Asian Research Centre for Advertisement, Journalism and Cartoons. n. d. 'Nehru on Indian Press'. Available at https://web.archive.org/web/20241223150840/http://www.sarcajc.com/nehru-on-indian-press.html (accessed February 2025).

Srivastava, Jatin and Enakshi Roy. 2016. 'Theoretical Perspectives: Issues in the Indian New Media Environment'. In *India Connected: Mapping the Impact of New Media*, edited by Sunetra Sen Narayan and Shalini Narayanan. New Delhi: Sage Books.

Taneja, Harsh. 2024. 'Who's Watching What on Indian TV? It's Complicated'. *360info.org*, 29 October. Available at https://thewire.in/media/whos-watching-what-on-indian-tv-its-complicated (accessed February 2025).

Telecom Regulatory Authority of India. 2012. 'Telecom Sector in India: A Decadal Profile'. New Delhi: National Council of Applied Economic Research.

———. 2023. 'Digital Inclusion in the Era of Emerging Technologies'. New Delhi: National Council of Applied Economic Research.

The Economic Times. 2020. 'BARC pauses weekly television ratings of all news channels for three months following TRP controversy', 15 October. Available at https://economictimes.indiatimes.com/news/india/barc-pauses-weekly-television-ratings-of-all-news-channels-for-three-months-following-trp-controversy/articleshow/78676757.cms?utm_source=contentofinterest&utm_medium=text&utm_campaign=cppst (accessed Februaru 2025).

The Hindu. 2012. 'In midnight drama, two AI crew members were held under IT Act', 24 November. Available at https://www.thehindu.com/news/national/In-midnight-drama-two-AI-crew-members-were-held-under-IT-Act/article15617537.ece (accessed February 2025).

———. 2013. 'India's requests for Web censorship increase', 27 April.

———. 2024. 'Whatsapp, Meta move Delhi high court against India's IT rules', 26 April. Available at https://www.thehindu.com/sci-tech/technology/whatsapp-meta-move-delhi-high-court-against-indias-it-rules/article68109392.ece (accessed May 2025).

———. 2025. 'Examining current provisions, need for new legal framework to regulate content: I&B Ministry', 22 February. Available at https://www.thehindu.com/news/national/examining-current-provisions-need-for-new-legal-framework-to-regulate-content-ib-ministry/article69250422.ece (accessed February 2025).

The Hindu Businessline. 2018. 'The Aadhaar of all things', 15 January. Available at https://www.thehindubusinessline.com/blink/cover/the-aadhaar-of-all-things/article64295146.ece (accessed February 2025).

———. 2021. 'What does the 26% FDI cap mean for digital news media?', 6 December. Available at https://www.thehindubusinessline.com/economy/policy/what-does-the-26-fdi-cap-mean-for-digital-news-media/article33132617.ece (accessed February 2025).

———. 2023. 'India's Internet subscribers increased to 881.25 million as of March-end: TRAI report', 21 August. Available at https://www.thehindubusinessline.com/info-tech/indias-internet-subscribers-increased-to-88125-million-as-of-march-end-trai-report/article67219636.ece (accessed February 2025).

The Indian Express. 2019 [1979]. 'Forty Years Ago: May 17, 1979'. Available at https://indianexpress.com/article/opinion/editorials/forty-years-ago-may-17-1979-5731843/ (accessed February 2025).

———. 2009. 'Report on Prasar Bharati functioning sent to PM: Soni', 15 October.

———. 2012. 'Mumbai police arrest cartoonist, slap sedition, cybercrime charges on him', 9 September. Available at https://www.thehindu.com/news/national/Mumbai-police-arrest-cartoonist-slap-sedition-cybercrime-charges-on-him/article12623053.ece (accessed February 2025).

———. 2023a. 'Prof held for sharing "defamatory" cartoons of Mamata acquitted', 21 January. Available at https://indianexpress.com/article/cities/kolkata/prof-held-for-sharing-defamatory-cartoons-of-mamata-acquitted-8394828/ (accessed February 2025).

———. 2023b. 'Press Bill passes LS, Thakur says "step to shed mentality of slavery"', 22 December. Available at https://indianexpress.com/article/india/press-bill-passes-ls-thakur-says-step-to-shed-mentality-of-slavery-9078171/ (accessed February 2025).

The Prasar Bharati (Broadcasting Corporation of India) Act, 1990. Available at https://www.indiacode.nic.in/bitstream/123456789/1959/3/A1990-25.pdf (accessed February 2025).

The Telegraph Online. 'deaf, dumb & dangerous', 26 March. Available at https://www.telegraphindia.com/india/deaf-dumb-amp-dangerous/cid/1475056 (accessed February 2025).

The Times of India. 2018. 'A spy state? Home ministry's blanket surveillance order must be tested against fundamental right to privacy', 23 December. Available at https://timesofindia.indiatimes.com/blogs/toi-editorials/a-spy-state-home-ministrys-blanket-surveillance-order-must-be-tested-against-fundamental-right-to-privacy/ (accessed February 2025).

The Tribune. 1998. 'Govt defends, Oppn slams Ordinance', 31 August. Available at https://www.tribuneindia.com/1998/98aug31/head3.htm (accessed February 2025).

The Wire. 2015. 'Four BJP Fellow Travellers Inducted to Prasar Bharati Board'. Available at https://thewire.in/media/four-bjp-fellow-travellers-inducted-to-prasar-bharati-board (accessed February 2025).

Thussu, Daya Kishan. 2016. 'Introduction'. In *India Connected: Mapping the Impact of New Media*, edited by Sunetra Sen Narayan and Shalini Narayanan. New Delhi: Sage Books.

Timmons, Heather. 2011. 'India Asks Google, Facebook to Screen User Content'. *New York Times*, 5 December. Available at https://archive.nytimes.com/india.blogs.nytimes.com/2011/12/05/india-asks-google-facebook-others-to-screen-user-content/ (accessed February 2025).

Tripurdaman Singh. n. d. 'How the First Amendment to the Indian Constitution Circumscribed Our Freedom and How it was Passed'. *Indian History Collective*. Available at https://indianhistorycollective.com/how-the-first-amendment-to-the-indian-constitution-circumscribed-our-freedoms-how-it-was-passed-amendmentoftheconstitution-nehruhistory-constitutional-gov-congressbill-parliamentarydemocracy/ (accessed February 2025).

UdayIndia. 2013. 'Why Should Section 66a Of The I.T. Act Not Be Deleted?', 5 January.

Verghese, B. G. 2005. *Warrior of the Fourth Estate: Ramnath Goenka of the Express*. New Delhi: Penguin Books.

———. 2010. *First Draft: Witness to the Making of Modern India*. Chennai: Westland/Tranquebar.

Yadav, Nikita. 2025. 'Bail for Indian professor arrested for comments on India-Pakistan conflict'. *BBC News*, 21 May. Available at https://www.bbc.com/news/articles/c93llyrrze7o (accessed May 2025).

Yasar, Kinza, Nick Barney and Ivy Wigmore. 2023. 'What is Deepfake Technology?' *Techtarget.com*. Available at https://www.techtarget.com/whatis/definition/deepfake (accessed February 2025).